all about Chalets

Contemporary
Mountain
Residences

all about Chalets

Contemporary Mountain Residences

Sibylle Kramer

BRAUN

Content

Inhalt

Preface

06

by Sibylle Kramer

Whether it is traditional architecture comprising a flat gable roof, wide roof overhangs and a solid, weathered wooden façade with a stone plinth, or a modern interpretation arranged in clear lines, with large panoramic windows, and fine details: the 67 masterfully designed chalets presented in this volume are as diverse and multifaceted as this. Yet no matter how they differ from one another, these houses, an exquisite selection from across the globe, have one common thread: they are all inspired by the beautiful nature surrounding them, the majestic mountains. A wide range of landscapes, rugged peaks, high altitudes, or gentle slopes, influence both the amount of sunlight and views, as well as the chalets' orientation, location, and layout. Again, and again, openings and panoramic windows are precisely placed, overlooking an enchanting valley, facing a striking rock or the beautiful wide horizon. These houses are characterized by the expression of deep affinity for nature and the wonderful promise it holds, as well as by their main feature, natural wood, which architects, and designers showcase in an artistic way. Whether it's solid, historical wood that carries the past or delicate, elaborate wooden lattices that channel natural light indoors, it's not just the façades that show the diversity of the material's use, but also the interiors, where concepts in wood are implemented with skilled craftsmanship. The selected chalets exude a warm, cosy, and homey atmosphere – sometimes contrasting, sometimes in harmony, bright or dark, modern, or classic, pure or in combination with other materials.

Von der traditionellen Bauweise mit flachem Satteldach, weitem Dachüberstand und robuster, wettergegerbter Holzfassade mit Steinsockel bis hin zur modernen Interpretation mit klarer Linienführung, großen Panoramafenstern und feinen Details – so vielfältig und facettenreich zeigen sich die in diesem Band präsentierten und meisterhaft entworfenen 67 Chalets. Doch so unterschiedlich diese weltweit ausgesuchten Häuser auch sind, stets eint sie die Auseinandersetzung mit der faszinierenden Naturwelt der kraftvollen Gebirge, die sie umgibt. Vielfältige Reliefformen, schroffe Gipfel, große Höhenlagen oder sanfte Hangneigungen beeinflussen sowohl den Einfall des Sonnenlichtes als auch die Qualität der Ausblicke und bestimmen damit die Ausrichtung, Lage und Raumkonfiguration der Chalets. Immer wieder werden Fensteröffnungen und Panoramascheiben präzise gesetzt – auf ein magisches Tal, einen markanten Felsen oder den wunderbar weiten Horizont. Der Ausdruck starker Naturverbundenheit und ihre zauberhafte Verheißung zeichnen diese Häuser ebenso wie die von natürlichem Holz dominierte Gestalt aus, die von den Architekten und Designern kunstvoll in Szene gesetzt wird. Ob massives historisches Holz, das die Geschichte der Vergangenheit erzählen kann oder feine, aufwendig gestaltete Holzgitter, die das Licht ins Innere lenken, nicht nur die Fassaden zeigen den vielfältigen Umgang mit dem Material, auch im Inneren überraschen handwerklich gekonnt umgesetzte Konzepte aus Holz. Mal aufregend kontrastreich, mal harmonisch ganzheitlich, hell oder dunkel, modern oder klassisch, pur oder in Kombination mit anderen Materialien – die ausgewählten Chalets strahlen immer eine warme, schützende und heimelige Atmosphäre aus.

Vorwort

Arla Luxury Home

08

Lech
Austria

Michael Ohneberg Architektur

09

Completion: 2020
Area: 330 m²
Number of Rooms: 14
Photos: Albrecht Imanuel Schnabel, Lichtbildner

The Arla Luxury Home is located in the Walser village of Lech, in Vorarlberg at 1,460 meters above sea level. The Arla is a classic chalet enhanced by contemporary architecture, which perfectly fits the village structure. In the pediment, delicate wickerwork spans the masonry pillars like a lattice girder and gives the chalet a unique look. Inside, this wickerwork provides plenty of sunlight and at the same time protects guests against unwelcome glimpses. Chalet Arla has a natural, lively and alpine look.

Das Arla Luxury Home steht im Walserdorf Lech in Vorarlberg auf 1.460 Meter Seehöhe. Das Arla ist ein klassisches Chalet im Kleid der zeitgenössischen Architektur, das sich einfühlsam in die Dorfstruktur eingliedert. Ein feines Flechtwerk im Giebelfeld überspannt die Mauerwerkspfeiler gleich einem Gitterträger und gibt dem Chalet ein sehr besonderes Erscheinungsbild. Im Innern bietet dieses Flechtwerk einen hohen Sonneneintrag und gleichzeitig einen Schutz vor ungewünschter Einsicht. Das Chalet Arla strahlt einen natürlichen, lebendigen und alpinen Charakter aus.

a **Interior view of the large panoramic window.**
Innenansicht großes Panoramafenster.

a

b

c

b **Exterior view of the Arla Luxury Home.**
Außenansicht Arla Luxury Home.

c **Interior view of the living room.**
Innenansicht Wohnzimmer.

d **First floor plan.**
Grundriss Erdgeschoss.

e **Second floor plan.**
Grundriss 1. Obergeschoss.

f **Interior view of a bedroom.**
Innenansicht Schlafzimmer.

g **View into kitchen with fireplace.**
Blick in die Küche mit Kamin.

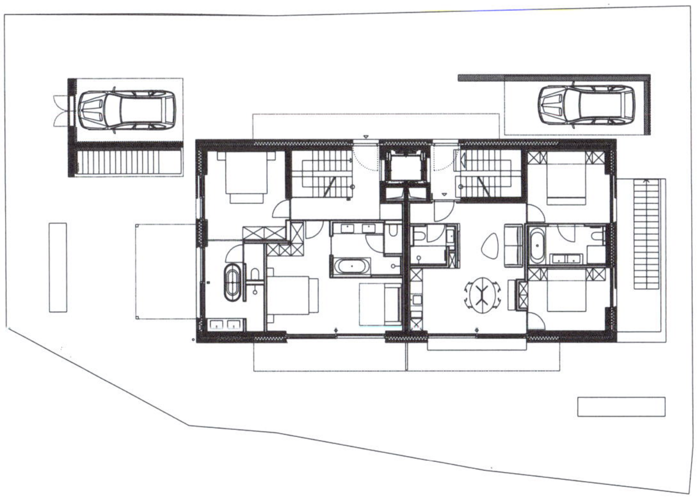

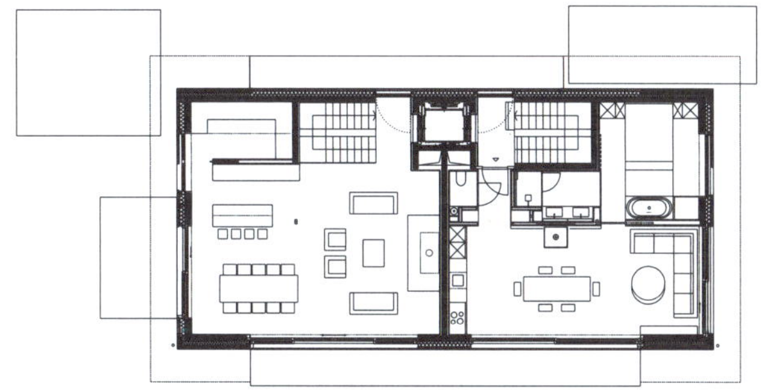

d e

f g

Baita MV

Madesimo Italy

Completion: 2021
Area: 135 m²
Number of Rooms: 3
Photos: Marcello Mariana

The chalet comprises a pre-existing part with a redesigned interior and two new extensions. The façade's structure meets the diverse functions of the house and has openings and wooden shutters that open onto the landscape or close off when the chalet is vacant. The house's design concept is based on the ambivalence of its two levels: the top level houses the open living area, that faces the wood terrace and the landscape; the lower level, used as sleeping area, provides instead more private spaces and has moderate openings. Carefully designed details such as the ceiling covered with wood slats characterize the interior throughout the house.

Der Bestandsbau des Chalets wurde neu gestaltet und um zwei neue Anbauten erweitert. Durch ihre Wandelbarkeit wird die Fassade der wechselnden Nutzung gerecht: Öffnungen und Holzläden geben den Blick auf die Landschaft frei oder verschließen sich, wenn das Chalet unbewohnt ist. Der Entwurf basiert auf der Ambivalenz der beiden Ebenen. Die obere Ebene beherbergt den offenen Wohnbereich, der sich zur Holzterrasse und zur Landschaft öffnet; die untere Ebene, die als Schlafbereich genutzt wird, bietet intimere Räume und maßvolle Öffnungen. Im gesamten Haus prägen gekonnt entworfene Details wie eine gefaltete Holzlamellen-Decke den Innenraum.

a **Interior view of the kitchen and living area on the second floor.** Innenansicht Küche und Wohnbereich im Obergeschoss.

a

b

c d

b **Exterior south-east view from below.**
Außenansicht Süd-Ost von unten.

c **Interior view of the master bedroom.**
Innenansicht Hauptschlafzimmer.

d **View into the stone shower with skylight.**
Blick in die Steindusche mit Oberlicht.

e **Baita cross section.**
Querschnitt Baita.

f **Panoramic view of the mountains from the upper terrace.**
Panoramablick auf die Berge von der oberen Terrasse.

e

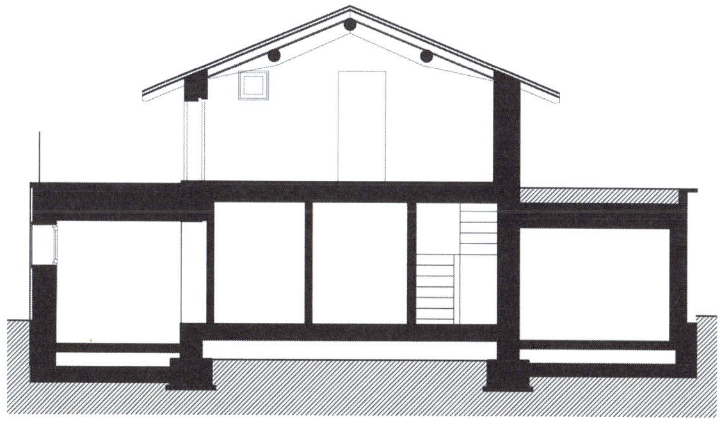

f

Ferienhaus HEUmond

Velden
Austria

LP architektur

Completion: 2020
Area: 170 m²
Number of Rooms: 4
Photos: Markus Rohrbacher

It is reduction and clearness of form in the context of the surroundings that sets this chalet apart from others. The new two-story structure is responding with its minimalist form language to the spotty neighbouring buildings. The reduced choice of materials – untreated larch wood and exposed concrete – underlines the design's purity. The house has two floors: downstairs are community and utility rooms, upstairs are bedrooms, bathrooms, and sauna. A dialog between inside and outside is created through openings that are positioned with great precision. Incisions in the building's cubature produce covered zones that extend the living areas to the outside.

Die Reduktion und die Klarheit der Form im Kontext zur Umgebung zeichnen dieses Chalet aus. Der zweigeschossige Neubau reagiert mit seiner einfachen Formsprache auf die punktuelle Nachbarbebauung. Die reduzierte Materialwahl – unbehandeltes Lärchenholz und Sichtbeton – unterstreicht die Klarheit des Entwurfs. Das Wohnhaus organisiert sich auf zwei Ebenen: unten die Gemeinschafts- und Funktionsräume, im Obergeschoss Schlaf- und Badezimmer sowie eine Sauna. Durch präzise gesetzte Öffnungen entsteht ein Dialog zwischen Innen und Außen. Einschnitte in der Gebäudekubatur erzeugen überdachte Bereiche, welche den Wohnbereich nach außen erweitern.

a **Interior view of the kitchen and living area with window seat.**
Innenansicht Küche und Wohnbereich mit Fenstersitzbank.

a

b

b **Exterior north-west view from the garden.**
Außenansicht Nord-West vom Garten.

c **Longitudinal section.**
Längsschnitt.

d **View of the roofed access area.**
Blick auf den gedeckten Zugangsbereich.

e **View of the bathroom and loggia on the second floor .**
Blick auf das Badezimmer und die Loggia im Obergeschoss .

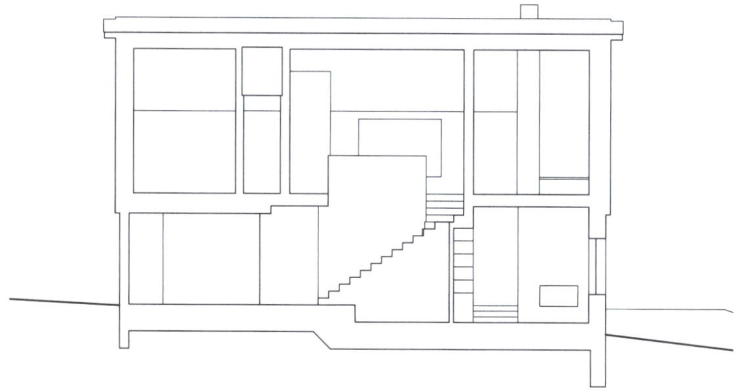

c

d e

Obomilla Waldchalets

South Tyrol
Italy

Completion: 2019
Area: 180 m²
Number of Rooms: 9
Photos: Gustav Willeit and Wolfgang Scherzer

The Obomilla Waldchalets in Meransen are located in an idyllic spruce forest and offer the best view of the Dolomites. The identity of the concept is based on the goal of meeting individual lifestyles, as well as on the local building culture. The fan shape of the ensemble offers privacy and varied views of nature. Although the individual units touch each other slightly at the corners, they do not merge into each other. This creates attractive niches that keep the site's original outlines visible. In reference to the adjacent forest, the interior of the chalets is made of natural and brushed spruce wood.

Die Obomilla Waldchalets befinden sich in Meransen in einer idyllisch gelegenen Fichtenwaldenklave mit bester Aussicht auf die Dolomiten. Der Wunsch nach individuellen Wohnformen sowie die örtliche Baukultur sind charaktergebend für das Entwurfskonzept. Die Fächerform des Ensembles schafft Privatsphäre und sorgt für unterschiedliche Ausblicke in die Natur. Die Einheiten berühren sich leicht an den Eckpunkten, verschmelzen jedoch nicht miteinander. Dadurch entstehen interessante Nischen, welche den ursprünglichen Geländeverlauf ablesbar lassen. Das Innenleben der Chalets ist in Analogie zum angrenzenden Wald in naturbelassenem und gebürstetem Fichtenholz ausgeführt.

a **Interior view of the dining room with panoramic window.**
Innenansicht Esszimmer mit Panoramafenster.

a

b

c

b **Rear exterior view of the chalets.**
Hintere Außenansicht der Chalets.

c **Staircase from below.**
Treppenhaus von unten.

d **Floor plan Obomilla Waldchalets.**
Grundriss Obomilla Waldchalets.

e **Side view chalet in surrounded by nature.**
Seitenansicht Chalet inmitten der Natur.

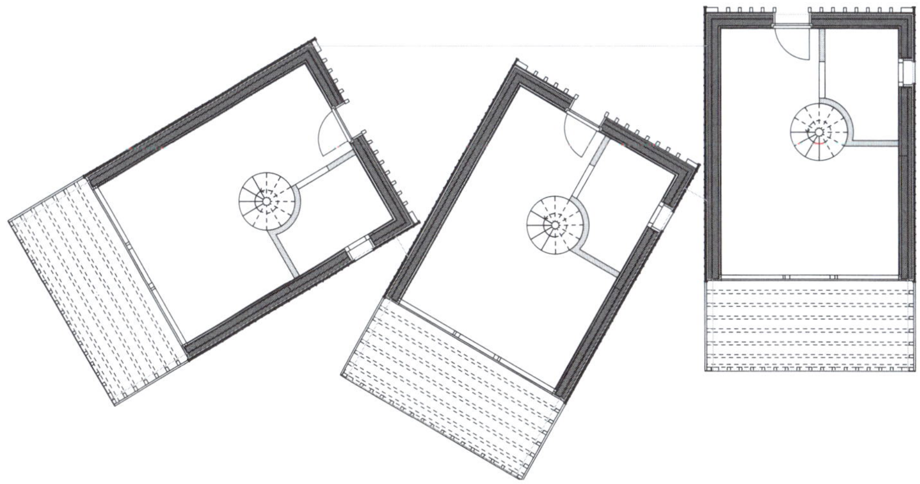

d

e

Mountain Cabin

South Tyrol Italy

24

Completion: 2020
Area: 35 m²
Number of Rooms: 3
Photos: Alex Filz

The Mountain Cabin, a design by Igor Comploi, is nestled in the woods of the Val Gardena. This black chalet has functional and modern furnishings by ruralurban and features an expressive combination of black ash and light spruce, as well as Swiss stone pine wood throughout the house. The high-quality kitchen made of granite and ash wood is the heart of the chalet. It is located right next to a large window that overlooks the forest and the secluded terrace. Next to the kitchen is the living room, which features light wood paneling and a sofa right by the window. The bed is located right by the window too, providing the most beautiful view on nature!

Mitten in den Wäldern des Grödner Tals liegt die Mountain Cabin, ein Entwurf von Igor Comploi. Das schwarze Chalet ist funktional und modern von ruralurban ausgestattet, die ausdrucksstarke Kombination von schwarzem Eschenholz und hellen Fichten- und Zirbenhölzern zieht sich durch das ganze Haus. Die hochwertige Küche aus Granit und Eschenholz ist der Mittelpunkt des Chalets. Sie grenzt an ein großes Fenster, das den Blick auf den Wald und gemütlichen Patio freigibt. Neben der Küche liegt die Stube mit heller Holztäfelung und einem direkt am Fenster stehenden Sofa. Auch im Schlafzimmer ist das Bett direkt an das Fenster gebaut – für schönste Aussichten in die Natur!

α **View of the covered porch.**
Blick auf die überdachte Veranda.

α

b

c d

b Interior view of the dining area with window seat.
Innenansicht Essbereich mit Fenstersitzbank.

c View into the living area.
Blick in den Wohnbereich.

d Bedroom with built-in bed.
Schlafzimmer mit Einbaubett.

e Detail of the bathroom.
Detail Badezimmer.

f Side view of the porch with mountain view.
Seitenansicht Veranda mit Blick auf die Berge.

e

f

Hütte Dolomiten

South Tyrol Italy

Bernd Gruber

Completion: 2019
Area: 180 m²
Number of Rooms: 4
Photos: Alexander van Berge
Styling: Bregje Nix

Nestled in a ski slope in the Dolomites, this mini chalet looks at first glance like a modest alpine hut. This modesty was a deliberate decision and mirrors the owner's desire for a private family retreat. The open plan living and dining area in the chalet's centre serves as meeting place and communication room. Lighting elements, together with the generous window front, are eye-catchers. As symbol of closeness to nature, waste wood is one of the main design elements and was used throughout the interior. The panoramic window offers a breath-taking view of the surrounding mountain landscape.

Inmitten einer Skipiste der Dolomiten wirkt dieses Mini-Chalet auf den ersten Blick wie eine einfache Almhütte. Diese bewusste Bescheidenheit spiegelt den Wunsch des Bauherrn nach einem privaten Rückzugsort für die Familie. Den Mittelpunkt der Hütte bildet der offen gestaltete Wohn- und Essbereich, der als Treffpunkt und als Raum für Kommunikation gedacht ist. Die Lichtelemente wirken zusammen mit der großzügigen Fensterfront als Blickfang. Als Symbol der Naturverbundenheit ist Altholz eines der tragenden Gestaltungselemente und wurde für den kompletten Innenausbau verwendet. Durch das Panorama-Fenster bietet sich ein atemberaubender Blick auf die umliegende Berglandschaft.

a **Living area with fireplace and a large window overlooking the Dolomites.**
Wohnbereich mit Kamin und großem Fenster mit Blick auf die Dolomiten.

a

b

c d

b **Exterior view of the chalet in the snow.**
Außenansicht des Chalets im Schnee.

c **Detail of the dining area's furnishings.**
Detail Einrichtung Essbereich.

d **Interior of the chalet completely covered with waste wood.**
Innenansicht des Chalets vollständig mit Altholz verkleidet.

e **Floor plan.**
Grundriss.

f **View of the living area from above.**
Blick auf den Wohnbereich von oben.

e

d

Larix Lodge in La Villa

South Tyrol
Italy

Completion: 2019
Area: 415 m²
Number of Apartments: 3
with a total of 5 bedrooms
Photos: Gerd Eder

Larix Lodge in La Villa is a contemporary designed vacation home with three apartments. The timber house atop a concrete basement was constructed using regional and sustainable materials. The apartments face southwest with large windows and an exterior space, providing views in all directions and have each private sauna. Natural materials from the region shape its face: the front was clad with rough sawn larch wood with a dark varnish. Inside, floors, walls, ceilings, and furniture are made of light-colored larch. The traditional materials are reinterpreted, complemented, or accentuated with colors.

Die Larix Lodge in La Villa ist ein zeitgenössisch konzipiertes Ferienhaus mit drei Apartments. Der Holzbau mit betoniertem Sockelgeschoss wurde aus regionalen und nachhaltigen Materialien konstruiert. Die Wohnungen öffnen sich nach Südwesten mit großen Fensterfronten und Außenraum und bieten Ausblicke in alle Himmelsrichtungen sowie jeweils eine eigene Sauna. Natürliche Materialien aus der Region bestimmen den Charakter: Die Fassade wurde mit sägerauem, dunkel lasiertem Lärchenholz verschalt. In den Innenräumen sind Fußböden, Wände, Decken und Möbel in heller Lärche gefertigt. Traditionelle Materialien werden neu interpretiert, ergänzt oder farbig akzentuiert.

a **Interior view of the dining and living area of the first floor apartment with windows overlooking garden.**
Innenansicht Ess- und Wohnbereich der Erdgeschosswohnung mit Fenstern zum Garten.

a

b

c d

b **View into the bedroom of the penthouse apartment.**
Blick ins Schlafzimmer der Dachgeschosswohnung.

c **Exterior view with snow from below.**
Außenansicht mit Schnee von unten.

d **Interior view of the living area with fireplace.**
Innenansicht Wohnbereich mit Kamin.

e **First and attic floor plans.**
Grundriss Erdgeschoss und Dachgeschoss.

f **Bedroom with panoramic view of the penthouse apartment.**
Schlafzimmer mit Panoramablick der Dachgeschosswohnung.

e

f

Chalet-2-Sphères

Canton Wallis
Switzerland

Completion: 2013, rebuild 2021
Area: 120 m²
Number of Rooms: 4
Photos: Christian Pfammatter and Sebastian Hatzfeldt

The name Chalet-2-Sphères derives from one of its upper floors dating from 1688, refurbished in 2013, and a decidedly contemporary ground floor. With regard to its reconstruction, a new basement was built in exposed concrete, as well as a new wood and steel substructure for the barn on the top floor. The interior design further emphasizes these two different spheres of the "old upstairs" and the "new downstairs". But despite all the differences in time and style, the two worlds are united by the cozy atmosphere with fantastic views throughout the chalet.

Der Name Chalet-2-Sphères leitet sich ab von einem Obergeschoss aus 1688, saniert 2013, und einem dezidiert modern gehaltenen Erdgeschoss. Die über 300 Jahre alte Scheune in Blockbauweise wurde zunächst Balken für Balken abgebaut. Für den Wiederaufbau wurde ein neues Untergeschoss in Sichtbeton, sowie für die Scheune im Obergeschoss eine neue Unterkonstruktion aus Holz und Stahl errichtet. Im Innenausbau werden diese zwei unterschiedlichen Sphären des „alten Oben" und „neuen Unten" noch stark akzentuiert. Doch trotz aller zeitlichen und stilistischen Unterschiede eint die beiden Welten die wohlige Atmosphäre mit phantastischen Ausblicken im ganzen Chalet.

a **Interior view of the living area with old stove.**
Innenansicht Wohnbereich mit altem Ofen.

a

b

c

b **Horizontal panoramic window in the dining room.**
Horizontales Panoramafenster im Esszimmer.

c **Exterior view with snow.**
Außenansicht mit Schnee.

d **Ground floor plan.**
Grundriss Erdgeschoss.

e **Children's bedroom with panoramic view.**
Kinderschlafzimmer mit Panoramablick.

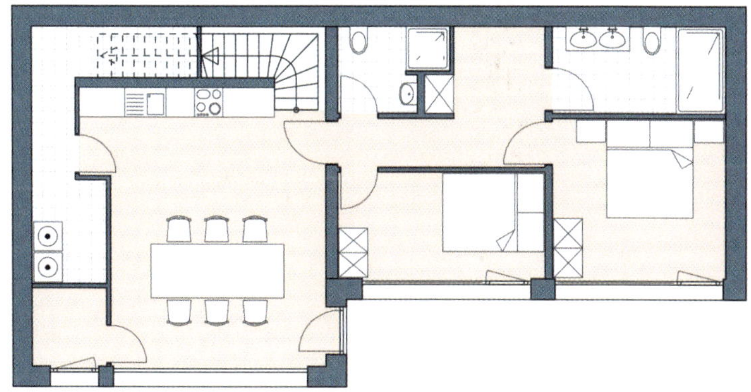

d

e

Haus H.

Zell am See
Austria

Completion: 2021
Area: 370 m²
Number of Rooms: 8
Photos: Foto-Studio Gretter

The alpine atmosphere can be enjoyed at any time of the year, as well as the sauna with a view and summer days at the private pool. Carefully planned for high standards, the house was erected on three complex levels. Built on a stone base, the façade made of old wood pays homage to the typical local materials and easily merges the house into the woody settlement. The color combinations, materials and finishes reflect the landscape of the region. The building's transparency provides a smooth transition between inside and outside, opening views from the dining room across the terrace to the pool and all the way to Lake Zell.

Zu jeder Jahreszeit das Ambiente der Berge, die Sauna mit Aussicht und Sommertage am eigenen Pool genießen. Auf drei komplexen Ebenen entstand ein durchdachtes Refugium für hohe Ansprüche. Die Altholzfassade auf einem Sockel aus Stein erweist den ortstypischen Materialien Referenz und garantiert eine unaufgeregte Allianz zur dicht bewaldeten Siedlung. Farbkombinationen, Materialien und Oberflächen nehmen Anklang an die Landschaft der Region. Die Durchlässigkeit des Gebäudes schafft einen fließenden Übergang zwischen innen und außen und ermöglicht Blicke vom Esszimmer über die Terrasse zum Pool bis hin zum Zeller See.

a **View into the living room with central fireplace.**
Blick in das Wohnzimmer mit zentralem Kamin.

a

b

c

b **Side view Haus H.**
Seitenansicht Haus H.

c **Interior view of a bedroom.**
Innenansicht Schlafzimmer.

d **Second floor plan.**
Grundriss 1. Obergeschoss.

e **Panoramic view from terrace with infinity pool.**
Panoramablick von der Terrasse mit Infinity-Pool.

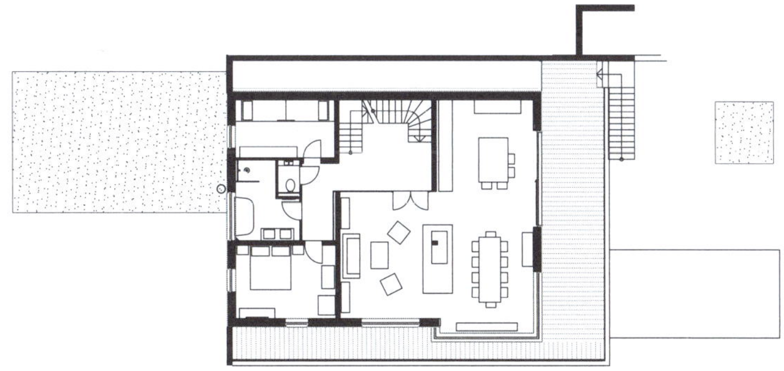

d

e

Tenne Chalets

South Tyrol Italy

Martin Gruber Architekt

Completion: 2020
Area: 240 m²
Number of Chalets: 4
Photos: Andreas Tauber

The luxurious Tenne Chalets breathe the energy of the forest. The strong connection to the landscape is based on the careful design of the transitions between architecture and nature. An unglazed skylight in the center of the building brings natural light and rain indoors, relating the chalets to the seasons and weather. Each of the four spacious chalets has two double bedrooms, an open fireplace, a kitchenette, a lounge, two bathrooms and a sunny communal terrace. The chalet service fulfills individual culinary wishes.

In den luxuriösen Tenne Chalets spürt man die Kraft des Waldes. Der unmittelbare Bezug zur Landschaft entsteht durch die sensibel gestalteten Übergänge zwischen Architektur und Natur. Ein unverglastes Himmelsfenster in der Mitte des Gebäudes lässt Licht und Regen hereinfallen und stellt den Bezug zu den Jahreszeiten und zum Wetter her. Die vier großzügigen Chalets verfügen jeweils über zwei Doppelzimmer, einen offenen Kamin, eine Küchenzeile, eine Lounge, zwei Badezimmer und eine gemeinsame Sonnenterrasse. Der Chalet-Service erfüllt individuelle Genusswünsche.

α **View of the mountains from the unglazed skylight.**
Blick auf die Berge aus dem unverglasten Dachfenster.

α

b

c d

b Living and dining room with stone fireplace.
Ess- und Wohnzimmer mit Steinkamin.

c Interior view to the bathroom.
Innenansicht zum Badezimmer.

d The chalet amidst nature.
Das Chalet inmitten der Natur.

e Interior view of a bedroom.
Innenansicht Schlafzimmer.

e

Bauernhaus

Feutersoey
Switzerland

Gehret Design

Completion: 2021
Area: 384 m²
Number of Rooms: 5
Photos: Phil Wenger Photography

The old farmhouse near Gstaad underwent a complete renovation and now shines in the splendor of a perfect mix of design, comfort, and technology. It was possible to save on materials and costs by highlighting the beauty of the raw materials. Minimalist, clean and by the use of wood as main material inside and outside, the result is modern comfort. Thanks to full-surface solar roofs, more electricity is currently generated than is needed, and beautiful roofscapes harmonize with the surroundings.

Das alte Bauernhaus nahe Gstaad wurde totalrenoviert und erstrahlt nun in einem idealen Mix von Design, Komfort und Technik. Indem die Schönheit der Rohstoffe in Szene gesetzt wurden, konnten Material und Kosten eingespart werden. Reduziert, klar und mit dem vorherrschenden Material Holz, innen wie außen, entsteht moderne Gemütlichkeit. Mit vollflächigen Solardächern wird nun mehr Strom als selbst gebraucht generiert und schöne Dachlandschaften integrieren sich in die Umgebung.

a **Interior view of the bedroom with panoramic window.**
Innenansicht Schlafzimmer mit Panoramafenster.

a

b

c

b **Large open living area and kitchen with a fireplace in the center.**
Großer offener Wohnbereich und Küche mit zentralem Kamin.

c **Exterior view Bauernhaus.**
Außenansich Bauernhaus.

d **View of the workspace.**
Blick auf den Arbeitsbereich.

e **Interior view of the dining area with balcony.**
Innenansicht Essbereich mit Balkon.

d

e

Chalet Mimi

Lech am Arlberg Austria

Completion: 2018
Area: 972 m^2
Number of Rooms: 20
Photos: Patrick Schwienbacher and Stefano Scatà

When designing Chalet Mimi, it was important to the architects to create traditional rooms that have a strong local connection, based on the Vorarlberg and alpine traditions. Simple, authentic materials are enhanced by local craftsmanship. Care for the material and its processing was at the forefront in the design of all furniture and details. The difference is in the details, in this case luxury is the care of the little things: specially designed traditional Vorarlberg embroidery patterns are being newly interpreted. The elements of hand embroidery are present in wall panels, lampshades and on cushions.

Ausgehend von der Tradition Vorarlbergs und der alpinen Tradition war es den Architekten bei der Gestaltung des Chalet Mimi wichtig, traditionelle Räume zu schaffen, die einen starken Ortsbezug haben. Einfache, ehrliche Materialien werden durch ortstypische Handwerkskunst veredelt. Der Respekt zum Material und seiner Verarbeitung stand bei der Konzeption sämtlicher Möbel und Details im Vordergrund. Der Unterschied liegt im Detail, Luxus ist hier die Sorgfalt der kleinen Dinge: Eigens entworfene traditionelle Vorarlberger Stickmuster werden neu interpretiert. Die handgestickten Elemente finden sich in Wandpaneelen, Lampenschirmen und auf Kissen wieder.

a **Interior view of dining area with antique tiled stove.**
Innenansicht Essbereichs mit antikem Kachelofen.

a

b

c

b **Interior view of living area with sitting niche.**
Innenansicht Wohnbereich mit Sitznische.

c **Bedroom and room with bunk beds.**
Schlafzimmer und Zimmer mit Kojenbetten

d **Attic floor plan.**
Grundriss Dachgeschoss.

e **Open bedroom and living area with fireplace.**
Offener Schlaf- und Wohnbereich mit Kamin.

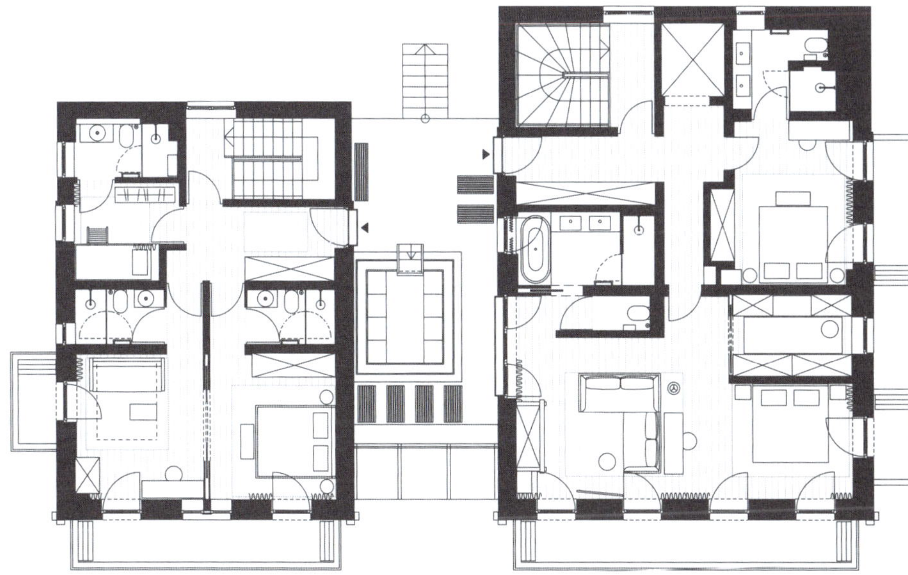

d

e

Mountain Chalet

Šumava National Park
Czech Republic

Completion: 2018
Area: 462 m²
Number of Rooms: 10
Photos: Tomáš Rasl

The chalet in the mountains, nestled in the South Bohemian countryside, includes two accommodation units. The concrete basement creates a solid base for the upper wooden structure combined with a timber joist ceiling. A massive granite plinth protects the traditionally cladded wooden façade on the lower level, the roof made of natural slate is in line with the typical local building tradition. In the main living areas, freestanding exposed concrete bodies house the sanitary facilities, which also have a static and microclimatic function. The surfaces of the plywood panels are largely treated with white semi-transparent oil finish to create a soft look.

Das in der südböhmischen Landschaft gelegene Bergchalet umfasst zwei Wohneinheiten. Der Betonsockel bildet eine solide Basis für die obere Holzkonstruktion in Kombination mit einer Holzbalkendecke. Ein massiver Granitsockel im unteren Bereich schützt die traditionell verkleidete Holzfassade, das Dach aus Naturschiefer entspricht der typischen lokalen Bautradition. In den Hauptwohnräumen befinden sich in freistehenden Sichtbetonkörpern die Sanitäranlagen, die auch eine bauliche und mikroklimatische Funktion erfüllen. Die Oberflächen der Sperrholz-Platten sind größtenteils mit weißer, halbtransparenter Ölfarbe behandelt, um eine sanfte Oberfläche zu erhalten.

a **Living room in the west with window seat during winter.**
Wohnzimmer auf der Westseite mit Fenstersitzbank im Winter.

a

b

c

b **Detail concrete core with stove.**
Detail Betonkern mit Ofen.

c **Side view Mountain Chalet from the meadow.**
Seitenansicht Mountain Chalet von der Wiese.

d **First floor plan.**
Grundriss Erdgeschoss.

e **Second floor plan.**
Grundriss 1. Obergeschoss.

f **Interior view children's bedroom with built-in sleeping alcoves.**
Innenansicht Kinder Schlafzimmer mit eingebauten Schlafnischen.

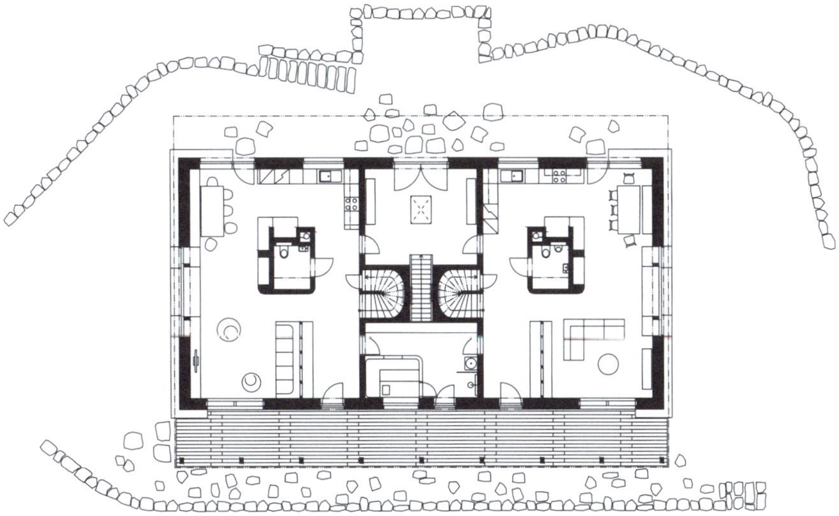

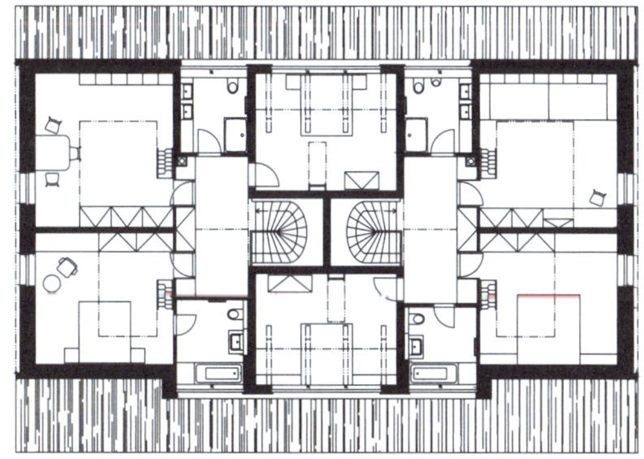

d e

f

Baumchalets Allgäu

Missen-Wilhams Germany

Completion: 2020
Area: 48 m²
Number of Chalets: 5
with 3 rooms each
Photos: Anna Fichtner

The five tree chalets are located amidst the green hills and shady woods of the Upper Allgäu. Facing north and to the sides, the chalets' façades are closed, facing south they are completely open. Sealed off from the outside by cool, dark sheet metal, the space inside is cozy and bright, shaped by wood and glass. Native spruce wood sets the tone for the overall design. Plenty of natural light enters the interior through large windows, the view sweeps out into nature. The kitchen, bathroom and sauna are on the first floor, two bedrooms on the second floor. The minimalist design language of the architecture puts nature in the center, enhancing its impact on guests.

Inmitten der grünen Hügel und schattigen Wälder des Oberallgäu sind die fünf Baumchalets entstanden. Die Chalets verschließen sich nach Norden und zur Seite, um sich auf der Südseite komplett zu öffnen. Nach außen hin kühl mit dunklem Blech abgeschottet, findet sich ein warmer, heller Raum im Innern, geprägt von Holz und Glas. Lokales Fichtenholz bestimmt das Design – die gläserne Front lässt viel Licht hinein und die Blicke hinaus in die Natur wandern. Im Erdgeschoss liegen Küche, Bad und Sauna, die zwei Schlafzimmer finden sich im Obergeschoss. Die einfache Formensprache der Architektur richtet den Fokus auf die Natur und lässt diese auf die Gäste wirken.

a **View of the terrace with whirlpool.**
Blick auf die Terrasse mit Whirlpool.

a

b

b **Exterior view back with its rustic shingles.**
Außenansicht Rückseite mit den rustikalen Schindeln.

c **Cross section.**
Querschnitt.

d **Panorama window on the chalet's south front.**
Panoramafenster an der Südfassade des Chalets.

e **Interior view living room with a hanging net seating area.**
Innenansicht Wohnzimmer mit abgehängtem Netzsitzbereich.

c

d e

Chalet W

Hokkaido
Japan

Completion: 2019
Area: 154.28 m²
Number of Rooms: 4
Photos: Daisuke Shima

Based on snow and local conditions, the project was designed to have a structure that combines a flat and a pitched roof. This way, it was possible to create a striking living/dining area that incorporates both the sloping surface, which serves as roof in the exterior, and the ceiling and walls of the interior. A small seating area offers a quiet space that doesn't interfere with the whole floor's openness. The airy interior design and calm color palette with lots of white and oak wood takes a back seat in favor of the owner's art collection. The materials used correspond with the surrounding birch trees and snowy landscape as well.

Ausgehend von den Schneeverhältnissen und den örtlichen Gegebenheiten wurde ein Volumen geplant, das ein Flachdach und ein Schrägdach kombiniert. So konnte ein markanter Wohn-/Essbereich geschaffen werden, der sowohl die schräge Fläche, die im Außenbereich als Dach dient, als auch die Decke und die Wände im Innenbereich einbezieht. Ein kleiner Sitzbereich schafft einen ruhigen Raum, ohne die Offenheit des gesamten Stockwerks zu stören. Die lichte Innenraumgestaltung und das ruhige Farbschema mit viel Weiß und Eichenholz nimmt sich zugunsten der Kunstsammlung des Besitzers zurück. Die verwendeten Materialien korrespondieren auch mit den umliegenden Birken und der verschneiten Landschaft.

a **Interior view of the living space with a view of the snowy landscape.**
Innenansicht Wohnzimmer mit Blick auf die verschneite Landschaft.

a

b

c

b **Interior view toward seating space.**
Innenansicht mit Blick auf den Sitzbereich.

c **Exterior view in snowy landscape.**
Außenansicht in Schneelandschaft.

d **First and second floor plans.**
Grundriss Erdgeschoss und 1. Obergeschoss.

e **Interior view of kitchen and dining room with long seat.**
Innenansicht Küche und Esszimmer mit langer Sitzbank.

d

e

Rainhof.bz

South Tyrol
Italy

Completion: 2015
Area: 500 m²
Number of Rooms: 10
Photos: Marion Lafogler

The 400-year-old Rainhof is a listed baroque farmhouse that underwent an extensive core renovation. Historical elements were restored, superfluous details were removed. Although the Rainhof has a historic exterior, it offers all the comforts of contemporary living. Whether furniture, wall coverings, floors, etc., wood is the predominant material, used in a modern and reduced way to have a cozy atmosphere everywhere, always bridging the gap between old and new.

Der 400 Jahre alte Rainhof ist ein denkmalgeschütztes, barockes Bauernhaus, das aufwendig kernsaniert wurde. Die historischen Elemente wurden restauriert, überflüssiges Beiwerk wurde entfernt. Von außen ganz im historischen Gewand, bietet der Rainhof allen Komfort und zeitgemäßes Wohnen. Möblierung, Wandvertäfelungen, Böden – Holz ist das vorherrschende Material, das modern und reduziert verarbeitet überall für eine behagliche Atmosphäre sorgt und immer wieder die Brücke zwischen Alt und Neu schlägt.

a **Dining area with balcony and overlooking the valley.**
Essbereich mit Balkon und Blick auf das Tal.

a

b

c

b **Interior view of the dining area and entrance area.**
Innenansicht Essbereich und Eingangsbereich.

c **Exterior north view with mountains background.**
Außenansicht Nord mit Bergen Hintergrund.

d **First and second floor plans.**
Grundrisse Erdgeschoss und Obergeschoss.

e **Bedroom with antique tiled stove.**
Schlafzimmer mit antikem Kachelofen.

d

e

Haus Ziegenhain

Bayrischzell
Germany

Completion: 2014
Area: 213 m²
Number of Rooms: 6
Photos: Sebastian Schels

Haus Ziegenhain is a long ridge house located in a beautiful setting on a steep slope of Bayrischzell overlooking the mountains. Wooden self-contained side walls support the timber-shingled roof, while the massive plinth area is of exposed concrete. The building has a simple cruciform structure that organizes the space. The transverse central area houses the kitchen with adjoining rooms and the dining area. The bedrooms and bathrooms are located on top of it. The two-storey living area is spacious. Large windows open the rooms to nature and bring a lot of natural light inside. The high-quality and reduced furnishings are characterized by a lot of wood.

Haus Ziegenhain liegt als langes Firsthaus in wunderschöner Lage an einem steilen Hang von Bayrischzell mit weitem Blick in die Berge. Geschlossene Seitenwände aus Holz tragen das holzverschindelte Dach, die massiven Sockelbereiche sind aus Sichtbeton. Eine einfache kreuzförmige Gebäudestruktur ordnet die Bereiche. Im quergesteckten mittleren Bereich findet man Küche mit Nebenräumen und Essplatz, darüber Schlaf- und Badezimmer. Der Wohnbereich ist zweigeschossig und großzügig. Große Fensterflächen öffnen die Räume zur Natur und lassen viel Licht herein. Viel Holz prägt die hochwertige und reduzierte Ausstattung.

a **Interior view of dining and living area with fireplace.**
Innenansicht Ess- und Wohnbereich mit Kamin.

a

b

c d

b **Exterior view of the chalet surrounded by snow.**
Außenansicht des Chalets inmitten von Schnee.

c **Interior view of the working area.**
Innenansicht Arbeitsbereich.

d **Bathtub with mountain view.**
Badewanne mit Bergblick.

e **First and second floor plans.**
Grundrisse Erdgeschoss und I. Obergeschoss.

f **Wooden façade detail.**
Holzfassade Detail.

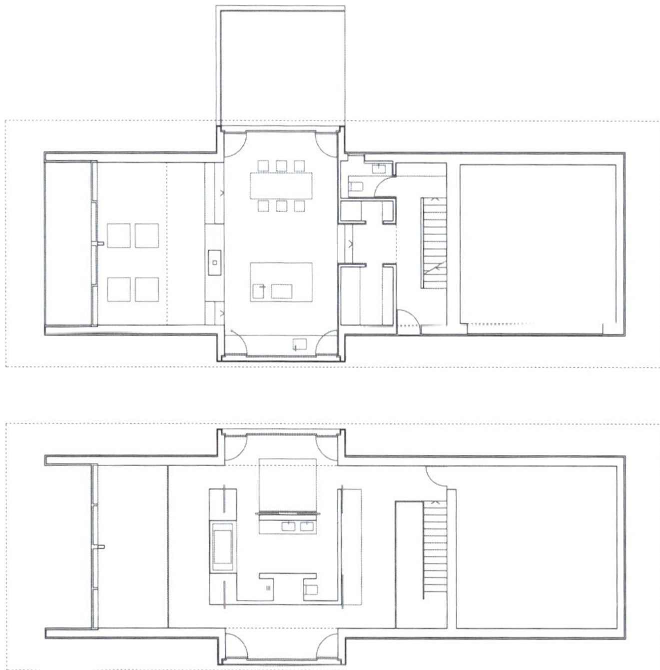

e

f

VY Cabin X

Hemsedal
Norway

Einar Jarmund & Co

Completion: 2017
Area: 94 m^2
Number of Rooms: 5
Photos: Sigurd Fandango and Knut Bry

The VY chalets are the result of blending modern building technology and Norwegian building tradition. Inspired by old Nordic house types, these homes feature typical protruding eaves, a sod roof with double pitch, extensive vertical panelling, as well as floor-to-ceiling windows and recessed terraces. Large windows bring the beauty of nature indoors, creating a unique atmosphere. The chalet's interior is in warm oak wood, the exclusive kitchen is at the heart of the open living area and opens up the view across the valley.

Die VY-Chalets sind das Ergebnis einer Mischung aus moderner Bautechnik und norwegischer Bautradition. Inspiriert von alten nordischen Gebäudetypen haben die Häuser die charakteristischen vorspringenden Traufen, ein Grassodendach mit doppelter Neigung, großzügige vertikale Verkleidungen sowie raumhohe Verglasungen und eingelassene Terrassen. Die großzügigen Fenster lassen die Schönheit der Natur in die Innenräume fließen und schaffen so eine ganz besondere Atmosphäre. Das Chalet ist mit warmem Eichenholz ausgestattet, die exklusive Küche befindet sich in der Mitte des offenen Wohnraums und gibt den Blick auf das schöne Tal frei.

a **Living space with natural light.**
Wohnraum mit natürlichem Licht.

a

b

c

b **Exterior view of the chalet with snow.**
Außenansicht des Chalets mit Schnee.

c **Bedroom with vertical windows.**
Schlafzimmer mit vertikalen Fenstern.

d **Floor Plan.**
Grundriss.

e **Generous outdoor terrace, a recessed part of the volume.**
Großzügige Außenterrasse als eingezogener Teil des Volumens.

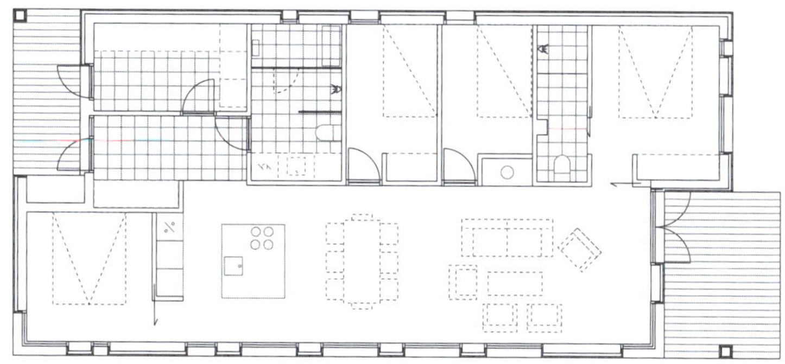

d

e

Rothaus

Andermatt
Switzerland

Completion: 2015
Area: 490 m²
Number of Rooms: 25
Photos: James Brittain

The Rothaus gets its name from its eye-catching and red-colored concrete exterior walls. Built on the existing foundations, the building was reimagined and realigned, and now has a direct view down into the valley. The hall emphasizes the old and new, while the other rooms have a quiet, structured relationship to the landscape beyond. Its concrete fronts protect the chalet's north and east elevations from the harsh north wind and have only a few small windows. The south and west fronts are clad in wood and have large windows. Over time, materials such as pigmented concrete, and laminated larch evolve a wide range of beautiful patinas.

Die markanten, roten Außenwände aus Beton geben dem Rothaus seinen Namen. Auf bestehenden Fundamenten wurde das Gebäude neu konzipiert und ausgerichtet, es schaut nun direkt auf das Tal hinunter. In der Halle sind die alten und neuen Koordinaten deutlich sichtbar, während die anderen Räume eine geordnete Beziehung zur Landschaft dahinter haben. Die Betonfassaden nach Norden und Osten schützen das Chalet vor dem rauen Nordwind und haben nur wenige kleine Fenster. Süd- und Westfassaden sind mit Holz bekleidet und haben große Fensteröffnungen. Die Materialien wie pigmentierter Beton and laminierte Lärche entwickeln im Laufe der Zeit eine reiche Patina.

a **Dining room aligned with the panoramic axis of the Ursner Valley.** Esszimmer ausgerichtet auf die Panoramaachse des Ursnertals.

b

c

b **Second floor bedroom with larch roof and large windows.**
Schlafzimmer im zweiten Stock mit Lärchendach und großen Fenstern.

c **Exterior view south side.**
Außenansicht Südseite.

d **First and second floor plans.**
Grundrisse Erdgeschoss und 1. Obergeschoss.

e **Interior view kitchen with wooden furniture and landscape view.**
Innenansicht Küche mit Holzmöbeln und Landschaftsblick.

f **View in the SPA with hot and cold pools.**
Blick in den Wellnessbereich mit Warm- und Kaltwasserbecken.

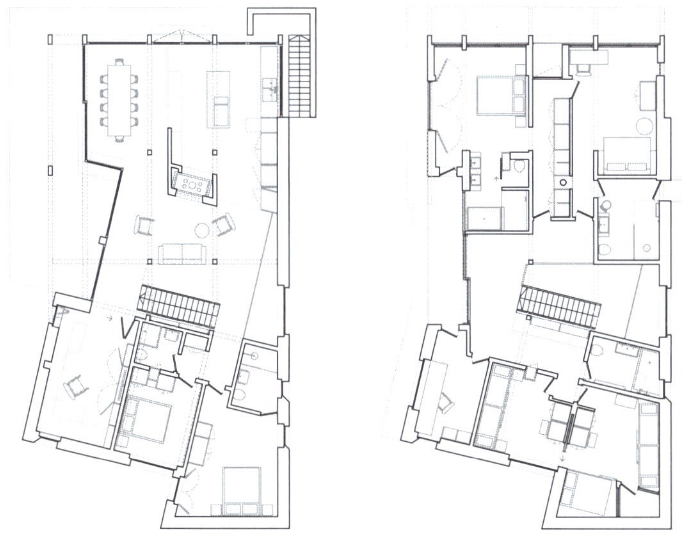

d

e f

Cortina Residence

Cortina d'Ampezzo Italy

Completion: 2017
Area: 105 m²
Number of Rooms: 5
Photos: Thomas Pagani

Cortina Residence is located on the upper floor of a listed Italian villa from the 1930s. When designing the chalet, the focus was on putting traditional materials in a modern light and reinforcing the house's pronounced connection with the surrounding natural landscape. The combination of the living room and the homely outdoor terrace, with large windows overlooking the mountains, gives the impression of having a single, large space. The mix of 100-year-old wainscoting matched with sleek, custom-made fixtures and few selected lights adds interesting contrasts between old and new.

Die Cortina Residence befindet sich im oberen Geschoss einer denkmalgeschützten, italienischen Villa aus den 1930er-Jahren. Traditionelle Materialien modern in Szene zu setzen und die starke Verbindung mit der umgebenden Naturlandschaft zu stärken, standen bei der Konzeption des Chalets im Fokus. Wohnzimmer und die wohnliche Außenterrasse wirken in Verbindung mit einer großen Fensterfläche und mit Blick auf die Berge wie ein einziger, großer Raum. Interessante Kontraste zwischen Alt und Neu entstehen in der Kombination von 100 Jahre alter Wandtäfelung mit schlichten, maßgefertigten Einbauten und reduzierten Leuchten.

a **Interior view of the dining area.**
Innenansicht Essbereich.

b **Detail of the window overlooking the panoramic terrace.**
Detail des Fensters mit Blick auf die Panoramaterrasse.

a b

c

d

c **Outdoor terrace with mountain views.**
Außenterrasse mit Bergpanorama.

d **Interior view of a bedroom.**
Innenansicht Schlafzimmer.

e **Cortina Residence floor plan.**
Grundriss Cortina Residence.

f **Floor plan and view of the terrace furniture.**
Grundriss und Ansichten Einrichtung Terrasse.

g **Interior view of the living area with fireplace.**
Innenansicht Wohnbereich mit Kamin.

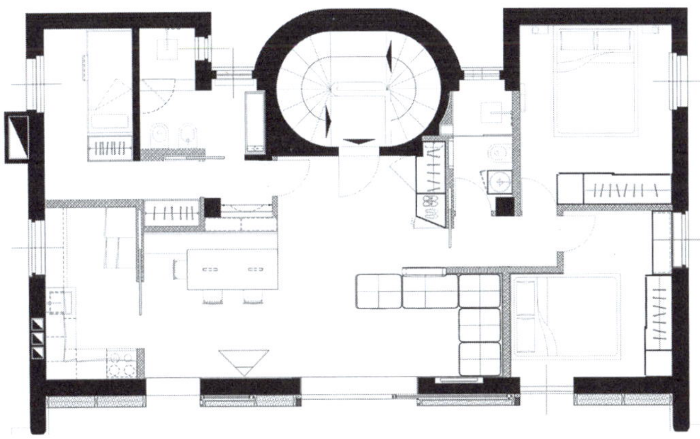

e f

g

Split View Mountain Lodge

Buskerud
Norway

Completion: 2013
Area: 130 m²
Number of Rooms: 8
Photos: Søren Harder Nielsen, Reiulf Ramstad Arkitekter

The chalet has a clear and clean-cut architectural style. Its light-coloured timber cladding on the exterior walls and roof, which will take on a grey patina over time, is in contrast with the elegant window profiles. The volume consists of a main body that follows the natural contours of the landscape and splits into two living zones. The annex is an extension of the main body, that has glass frontages at the end walls contributing to its distinctive split views. The chalet carries on Norwegian building traditions in form and materiality, responding to the landscape's context.

Das Chalet strahlt eine klare und schnörkellose Architektur aus. Die helle, durchgehende Holzverkleidung an den Außenwänden und am Dach wird mit eleganten Fensterprofilen kontrastiert und mit der Zeit eine graue Patina annehmen. Das Volumen besteht aus einem Hauptkörper, der den natürlichen Konturen der Landschaft folgt und sich in zwei Wohnbereiche aufteilt. Der Anbau ist in Verlängerung des Hauptkörpers angeordnet. Das Chalet lässt mit seinen verglasten Stirnwänden die drei charakteristisch geteilten Ansichten entstehen. Es führt die norwegischen Bautraditionen in Form und Materialität fort, und reagiert auf den Kontext der Landschaft.

a **View into the kitchen and living area with mountain panorama.**
Blick in die Küche und Wohnbereich mit Bergpanorama.

a

b c

d

b **Interior view of a bedroom.**
Innenansicht Schlafzimmer.

c **Dining area with panoramic window and alcove.**
Essbereich mit Panoramafenster und Alkoven.

d **Interior view of the kitchen.**
Innenansicht Küche.

e **First floor plan.**
Grundriss Erdgeschoss.

f **Exterior view with snow.**
Außenansicht mit Schnee.

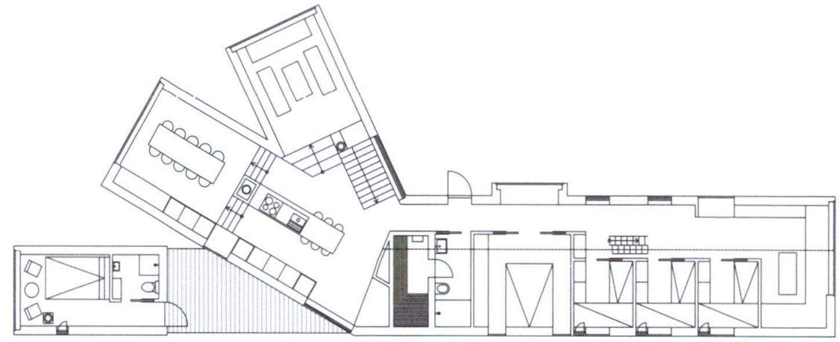

e

f

Chalet Südtirol

South Tyrol Italy

Completion: 2017
Area: 190 m²
Number of Rooms: 5
Photos: James Strokes

When an architect and a designer remodel their own chalet, a gorgeous composition can come to life, as Willo Blome and Barbara Nöcker-Blome show. They fuse the mountain coziness with a modern style. The original house was small; two rooms, a kitchen, and a fireplace, but with a fantastic view of the mountains. On the first floor of the old building, they built a new one with a pitched roof. The living room has an open kitchen in black steel, a sculptural staircase and a gable with glass giving it a timeless modern touch, while the floor and walls are made of old recycled wood.

Wenn eine Architektin und ein Designer das eigene Chalet umbauen, kann eine wunderbare Komposition entstehen, wie Willo Blome und Barbara Nöcker-Blome zeigen. Sie vereinen die Berggemütlichkeit mit modernem Stil. Das ursprüngliche Haus war klein; zwei Zimmer, eine Küche und ein Kamin, aber mit einem fantastischen Blick auf die Berge. Auf den ersten Stock des Altbaus setzten sie ein neues Stockwerk mit Satteldach. Das Wohnzimmer mit der offenen Küche aus schwarzem Stahl, der skulpturalen Treppe und dem Giebel mit Glas verleiht einen zeitlos modernen Touch, während altes recyceltes Holz für den Boden und die Wände verwendet wurde.

a **Interior of the living room with fireplace and panoramic window.**
Innenansicht Wohnzimmer mit Kamin und Panoramafenster.

a

b c

d e

b Interior view of the staircase.
Innenansicht Treppe.

c View into the dining area with balcony.
Blick in den Essbereich mit Balkon.

d Interior view of a bedroom.
Innenansicht Schlafzimmer.

e Bathroom with sauna.
Badezimmer mit Sauna.

f Interior of the kitchen with cooking island and horizontal window.
Innenansicht Küche mit Kochinsel und horizontalem Fenster.

f

Maison aux Jeurs

Les Jeurs Switzerland

Completion: 2013
Area: 150 m²
Number of Rooms: 5
Photos: Joël Tettamanti

The chalet in Les Jeurs uses shapes and proportions of the neighboring traditional buildings. Like the traditional granaries of the Valais, it has a wooden structure that is supported by a stone plinth. Since a single, large space would have disrupted the harmony of the building's proportions, it is divided into two parts, joining on the mountainside and separate at 45 degrees towards the valley. It has two large windows which let the landscape stream into the building. All the interior is made of untreated fir wood, while the façade is clad in tinted larch wood, in the style of traditional mountain huts.

Das Chalet in Les Jeurs arbeitet mit Form und Maßstab der benachbarten, traditionellen Gebäude. Wie ein Walliser Getreidespeicher besteht es aus einem Steinsockel auf dem ein Volumen aus Holz aufgeständert ist. Da ein einzelnes, großes Volumen die Harmonie der Maßstäbe gestört hätte, ist das Gebäude in zwei Teile gegliedert, die auf der Bergseite miteinander verbunden und zum Tal hin durch einen Winkel von 45 Grad getrennt werden. Zwei große Fenster lassen die Landschaft in das Gebäude fließen. Die Innenräume sind komplett mit unbehandeltem Tannenholz ausgestattet, die Fassade ist in Anlehnung an traditionelle Berghütten mit getöntem Lärchenholz verkleidet.

a **Interior view of the entrance on the mountain side.**
Innenansicht Eingangsbereich an der Bergseite.

a

b

c

b Side view of Maison aux Jeurs.
Seitenansicht Maison aux Jeurs.

c Interior with panoramic view of the mountains.
Innenansicht mit Panoramablick auf die Berge.

d Basement floor plan.
Grundriss Untergeschoss.

e First floor plan.
Grundriss Erdgeschoss.

f Second floor plan.
Grundriss Obergeschoss.

g Exterior view of the chalet in snowy landscape.
Außenansicht Chalet umgeben von verschneiter Landschaft.

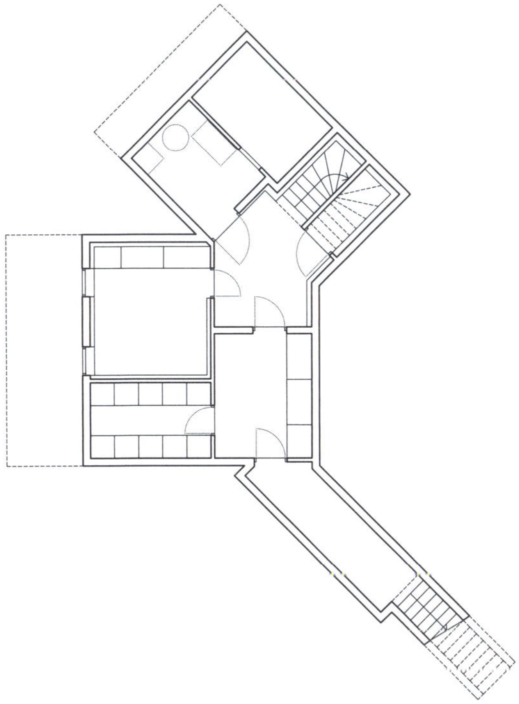
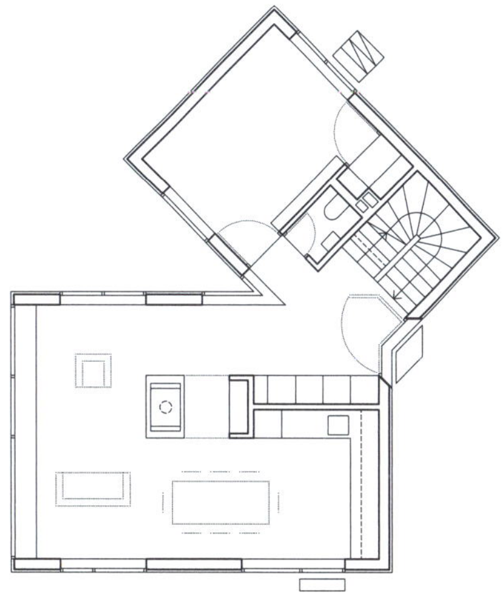
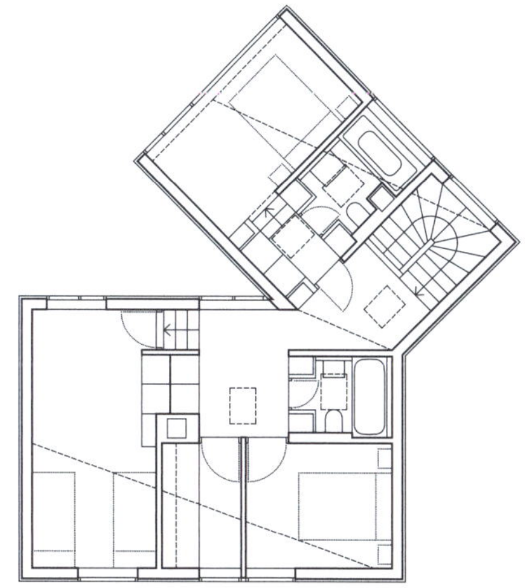

d e f

g

Stefan Glowacz
Mountain Houses
CHALET

Grainau
Germany

Completion: 2021
Area: 180 m²
Number of Rooms: 5
Photos: Tanja Valérien

The Stefan Glowacz CHALET is a new organic timber house. The detached vacation home with garden is in the heart of the romantic alpine village of Grainau, not far from Garmisch-Partenkirchen, right at the foot of Germany's highest mountain, the Zugspitze. This special hideaway blends sustainability, tradition, modernity, and design. The Mountain House has two bedrooms, two bathrooms, a large living area, gas fireplace, sauna, and a large yoga room, which can also be perfectly used for lectures and as a business room. A sunny south-facing terrace and its garden offer a wonderful, unobstructed view of the majestic alpine panorama.

Das Stefan Glowacz CHALET ist ein neu gebautes Bio-Holzhaus. Das freistehende Ferienhaus mit Garten liegt mitten im romantischen Alpendorf Grainau, unweit von Garmisch-Partenkirchen, direkt am Fuße von Deutschlands höchstem Berg, der Zugspitze. Dieses besondere Hideaway vereint Nachhaltigkeit, Tradition, Moderne und Design. Das Mountain House verfügt über zwei Schlafzimmer, zwei Bäder, einen großen Wohnbereich, Gas-Kamin, Sauna und einen großen Yoga-Raum, der auch als Vortrags- und Businessraum perfekt genutzt werden kann. Eine sonnige Südterrasse und der Garten bieten einen herrlichen, unverbauten Blick auf das Alpenpanorama.

a **Interior view of the living area with fireplace.**
Innenansicht Wohnbereich mit Kamin.

a

b

c d

b Interior view of the kitchen with black steel glass wall.
Innenansicht Küche mit Schwarzstahl-Glaswand.

c Dining area with wooden bench.
Essbereich mit Holzbank.

d Detail of the wood façade made of steamed and chopped spruce.
Detail der Fassade aus gedämpfter und gehackter Fichte.

e Interior view of the wooden staircase.
Innenansicht der Holztreppe.

f Bedroom with vintage furniture.
Schlafzimmer mit Vintage-Mobiliar.

e

f

Stefan Glowacz
Mountain Houses
VINTAGE

Grainau
Germany

Tanja Valérien-Glowacz

Completion: 1936 construction,
2010 renovation.
Area: 170 m²
Number of Rooms: 8
Photos: Tanja Valérien
and Bärbel Miebach

The four-star rated VINTAGE House of Stefan Glowacz Mountain Houses, built in 1936, offers plenty of space on 170 square meters and has a separate garden house. The vacation home is located directly at the foot of the Zugspitze, only a minute walk from the Zugspitze cable car. This unique vintage chalet is decorated in a modern style with shabby chic and industrial furniture. The main house has a beautiful open plan kitchen/living room, which leads into a large dining room with fireplace and a sunny living room in the conservatory. A large terrace in front of the living room faces south and offers a breathtaking view of the Zugspitze.

Das mit vier Sternen klassifizierte VINTAGE Haus der Stefan Glowacz Mountain Houses, erbaut 1936, bietet auf 170 qm viel Platz und verfügt zusätzlich über ein separates Gartenhaus. Das Ferienhaus liegt direkt am Fuße der Zugspitze, nur eine Gehminute zur Zugspitzbahn entfernt. Dieses besondere Chalet im Vintage Style ist modern mit Möbeln im Shabby Chic und Industrial Style eingerichtet. Im Haupthaus gibt es eine wunderschöne, offene Wohnküche übergehend in ein großes Esszimmer mit Kaminofen und ein sonniges Wohnzimmer im Wintergarten. Vor dem Wohnzimmer liegt auf der Südseite eine große Terrasse, mit atemberaubendem Blick auf die Zugspitze.

a **Interior view of the living room in the winter garden.**
Innenansicht Wohnzimmer im Wintergarten.

b

c d

b **General view of the two Stefan Glowacz Mountain Houses CHALET (right) and VINTAGE (left).**
Gesamtansicht der beiden Stefan Glowacz Mountain Houses CHALET (rechts) und VINTAGE (links).

c **Interior view of the dining area.**
Innenansicht Essbereich.

d **Exterior detail of the entrance door.**
Außendetail Eingangstür.

e **Interior view of a bedroom.**
Innenansicht Schlafzimmer.

e

Chalet MKN

Salvan
Switzerland

Completion: 2021
Area: 201 m²
Number of Rooms: 8
Photos: Christophe Voisin

Chalet MKN comes from a long-held dream of a Scandinavian family of four in the Swiss Alps. Hence, the overall design of the chalet is inspired by the family's roots and the surrounding breathtaking mountain scenery. The property is perfectly oriented towards the Rhone Valley, offering stunning views that frame the chalet in all common areas and rooms, while the distribution and ancillary spaces are all oriented uphill, opposite the driveway. The color and material concept of the chalet responds to the surrounding nature, enhancing the feeling of being in the mountains and staying in touch with nature.

Das Chalet MKN ist ein lang gehegter Traum einer vierköpfigen skandinavischen Familie in den Schweizer Alpen. Das Gesamtdesign des Chalets ist daher von den Wurzeln der Familie und der umliegenden, atemberaubenden Berglandschaft inspiriert. Das Grundstück ist perfekt auf das Rhonetal ausgerichtet und bietet eine atemberaubende Aussicht, die das Chalet in allen Gemeinschaftsbereichen und Zimmern einrahmt, während die Verteilungs- und Nebenräume alle bergauf, gegen die Zufahrt ausgerichtet sind. Das Farb- und Materialkonzept des Chalets ist so gestaltet, dass es auf die umgebende Natur reagiert und das Gefühl stärkt, in den Bergen zu sein und in Verbindung mit der Natur zu bleiben.

a **Interior view of the dining and living area with terrace.**
Innenansicht Ess- und Wohnbereich mit Terrasse.

a

b

c

b **Kitchen with peninsula and view of the entrance area.**
Küche mit Halbinsel und Blick auf den Eingangsbereich.

c **Exterior view from the garden.**
Außenansicht aus dem Garten.

d **Lower floor plan.**
Grundriss Untergeschoss.

e **First floor plan.**
Grundriss Erdgeschoss.

f **Attic floor plan.**
Dachgeschoss.

g **View of the valley from the covered terrace.**
Blick auf das Tal von der überdachten Terrasse.

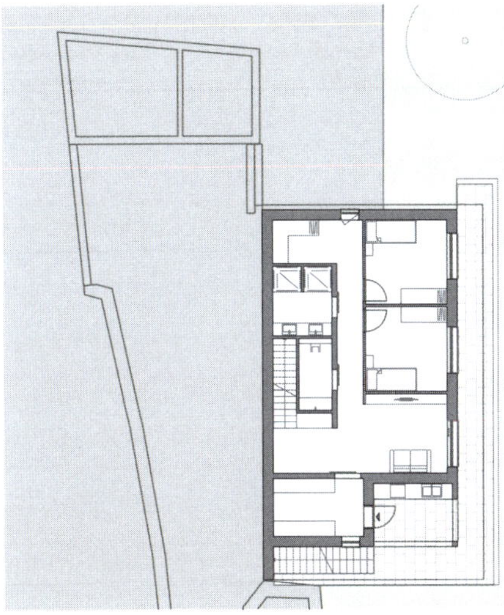

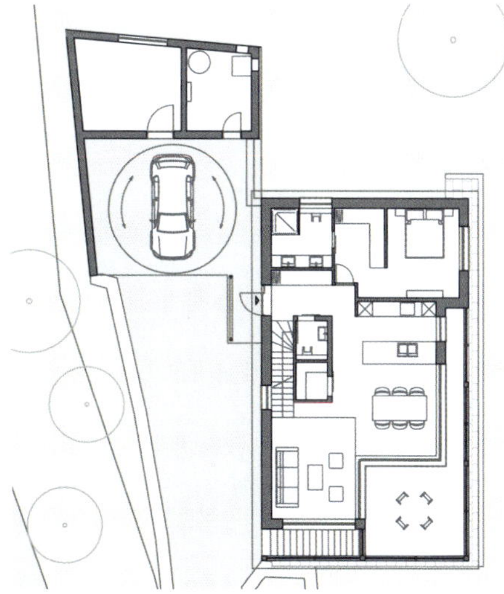

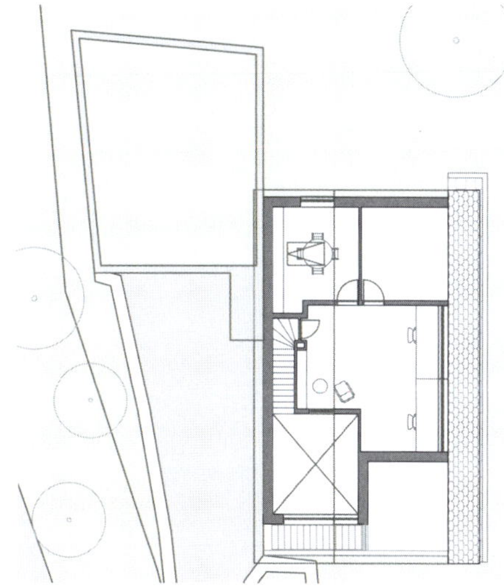

d e f

g

Mineral Lodge

Villaroger France

Completion: 2012
Area: 371 m^2
Number of Rooms: 9
Photos: Nicolas Borel

Mineral Lodge is a new building embedded in existing ruins without touching them. This creates an intermediate space that bridges past and present. Unlike conventional chalet design, Mineral Lodge relies on plenty of natural light and features window glass of exceptional quality. Backed by geothermal heating, the chalet is designed to provide a high level of living comfort. A heat pump channels water into three boreholes in the rock, where temperature is constant all year round. Both heating and cooling supply of the chalet are invisible, because it uses floor heating and double-flux ventilation.

Die Mineral Lodge ist ein neuer Bau, der in vorhandene Ruinen eingebettet wurde, ohne diese zu berühren. So entsteht ein zwischengelagerter Raum, der eine Brücke zwischen Vergangenheit und Gegenwart schlägt. Im Gegensatz zum konventionellen Chaletdesign setzt die Mineral Lodge auf viel Tageslicht und verwendet Fensterglas von besonderer Qualität. Unterstützt von einer geothermalen Heizung wird in dem Chalet ein hoher Wohnkomfort geschaffen. Eine Wärmpumpe schleust Wasser in drei Bohrungen im Felsen, wo die Temperatur das ganze Jahr über stabil ist. Dank einer Fußbodenheizung sowie einer Double-Flux-Belüftung ist sowohl die Wärme- als auch die Kühlzufuhr des Chalets unsichtbar.

a **Dining area with large windows on the original stone walls.**
Essbereich mit großen Fenstern an den originalen Steinmauern.

a

b

c d

b **Interior view of the second floor overlooking the surrounding countryside.**
Innenansicht Obergeschoss mit Blick auf die umliegende Landschaft.

c **View of the staircase.**
Blick auf die Treppe.

d **Interior view of the kitchen.**
Innenansicht Küche.

e **Mineral Lodge Axonometry.**
Axonometrie Mineral Lodge.

f **Exterior view in the evening.**
Außenansicht mit Abendstimmung.

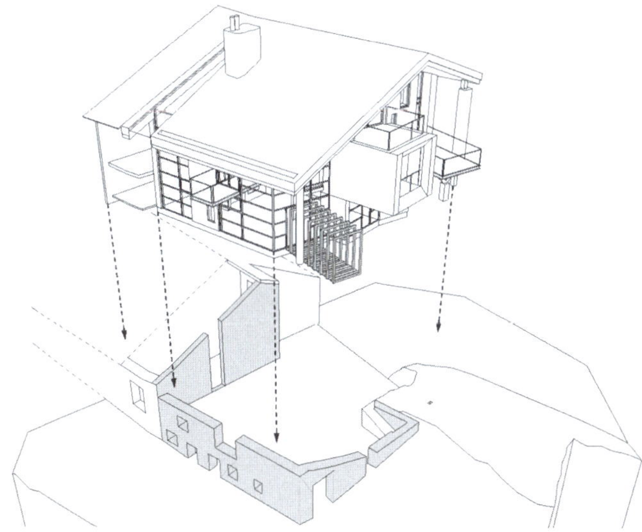

e

f

Bosco Diffuso

Saint Moritz Switzerland

Completion: 2017
Area: 500 m²
Number of Rooms: 14
Photos: Mattia Aquila

Overlooking the lake, in the middle of a clearing, this three-story chalet has become the vacation home of a young family. The emphasis was on a homey atmosphere. This coziness is created by lots of wood on the floors and walls and elaborately paneled ceilings. The furniture and furnishings also follow this idea, creating a warm, inviting atmosphere that goes hand in hand with a minimal color concept. Individual details such as cowhides or walls with Wall&decò wallpaper depicting the orography of the Lepontine Alps accentuate the decor.

Mit Blick auf den See, inmitten einer Lichtung, ist dieses dreistöckige Chalet zum Feriendomizil einer jungen Familie geworden. Im Focus stand die Kreation einer behaglichen Atmosphäre und so sorgt der Einsatz von viel Holz bei Boden- und Wandbekleidung sowie teilweise aufwendig vertäfelten Decken für gemütliche Stimmung. Auch die Möblierung und Dekoration folgt diesem Gedanken und erzeugt eine warme, einladende Athmosphäre, die mit reduziertem Farbkonzept einher geht. Individuelle Details wie der Einsatz von Kuhfellen oder eine Wandgestaltung mit Wall&decò-Tapete, die die Orographie der Lepontinischen Alpen darstellt, setzen gelungene Akzente.

a **Interior view of the living room with fireplace.**
Innenansicht Wohnzimmer mit Kamin.

a

b

c d

b **Living room with old wood paneling.**
Wohnzimmer mit altem Holz verkleidet.

c **Dining area with wood paneling and colored lamp.**
Essbereich mit Holzverkleidung und farbiger Lampe.

d **Bedroom with forest view.**
Schlafzimmer mit Waldblick.

e **Second floor plan.**
Grundriss 1. Obergeschoss.

f **Private indoor swimming pool with panoramic view.**
Privates Innenschwimmbad mit Panoramablick.

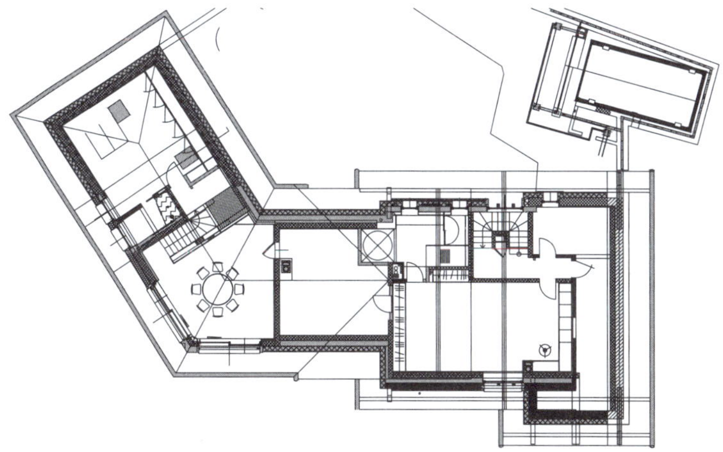

e

f

La Chalette

Lenzkirch
Germany

Completion: 2020
Area: 43 m²
Number of Rooms: 2
Photos: Roland Halbe

A wooden shed next to a listed farm from 1659 at an altitude of 1,000 meters in the Upper Black Forest was converted into a small single-family house. Its skin as well as the characteristics of the original house were preserved. There are only minor changes indicating conversion. The existing openings and the huge door of the barn are generously glazed. Inside, the building was insulated and covered with native silver fir cladding. This material was also used for the interior fittings as well for the flooring, just in line with the consistent implementation of the harmonious color and materials concept.

Im Hochschwarzwald auf 1.000 m Höhe wurde neben einem denkmalgeschützten Bauernhof von 1659 ein Holzschuppen in ein kleines Einfamilienhaus umgebaut. Dabei blieben die äußere Hülle und der Charakter des ursprünglichen Gebäudes erhalten. Lediglich kleine Eingriffe lassen erkennen, dass hier ein Umbau stattgefunden hat. Die bereits vorhandenen Öffnungen sowie das große Scheunentor wurden großzügig verglast. Im Inneren wurde das Gebäude gedämmt und mit einer heimischen Weißtannen-Verkleidung versehen. Im Sinne der konsequenten Umsetzung des harmonischen Farb- und Materialkonzeptes wurde die Weißtanne auch für die Einbauten und als Bodenmaterial verwendet.

a **View of the sitting area in the kitchen.**
Blick auf die Sitzecke in der Küche.

b **Exterior view from the garden.**
Außenansicht vom Garten.

a b

c

d

c **Interior view of the living area with horizontal narrow window.**
Innenansicht Wohnbereich mit horizontalem schmalem Fenster.

d **Bathroom with bathtub.**
Badezimmer mit Badewanne.

e **Longitudinal section.**
Längsschnitt.

f **View into the living area with terrace.**
Blick in den Wohnbereich mit Terrasse.

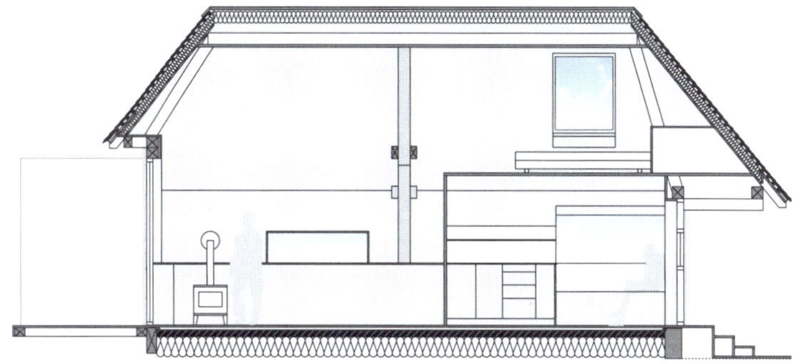

e

f

Cascina

Alte Langhe Italy

Completion: 2020
Area: 409.5 m^2
Number of Rooms: 20
Photos: Francesca Iovene

A home and studio came to life through the conversion of a 200-year-old historic farmhouse in Piedmont. With an eye on the region and a focus on sustainability, much of the original substance of the building was reused, including the original tiles and the old gnarled, wooden structure of the roof, which was left where it was to preserve the original tectonics. The warm look of the façade's handcrafted plaster echoes the identity of the building materials inside and, along with terracotta, wood, and brick, makes up for the structured range of materials that is characteristic to the entire house.

Im Piemont entstand durch den Umbau eines 200 Jahre alten historischen Bauernhofs ein Wohnhaus und Atelier. Mit Blick auf die Region und Fokus auf Nachhaltigkeit wurde ein Großteil der ursprünglichen Bausubstanz wiederverwendet, einschließlich der ursprünglichen Fliesen und der alten, knorrigen Holzkonstruktion des Daches, die an Ort und Stelle belassen wurde, um die ursprüngliche Tektonik zu erhalten. Die warme Textur des handgefertigten Putzes der Fassade setzt die Materialsprache im Inneren fort und schafft zusammen mit Terracotta, Holz und Ziegeln eine strukturierte Materialpalette im gesamten Haus.

a **View of the living room with large windows.**
Blick ins Wohnzimmer mit großen Fenstern.

a

b

c d

b Interior view of study on the second floor.
Innenansicht Arbeitszimmer im ersten Obergeschoss.

c Second floor study entrance.
Eingang zum Arbeitszimmer im ersten Obergeschoss.

d Interior view of the kitchen with landscape view.
Innenansicht Küche mit Landschaftsblick.

e Ground floor plan.
Grundriss Erdgeschoss.

f Exterior view of the east elevation surrounded by snow.
Aussenansicht der Ostfassade umgeben von Schnee.

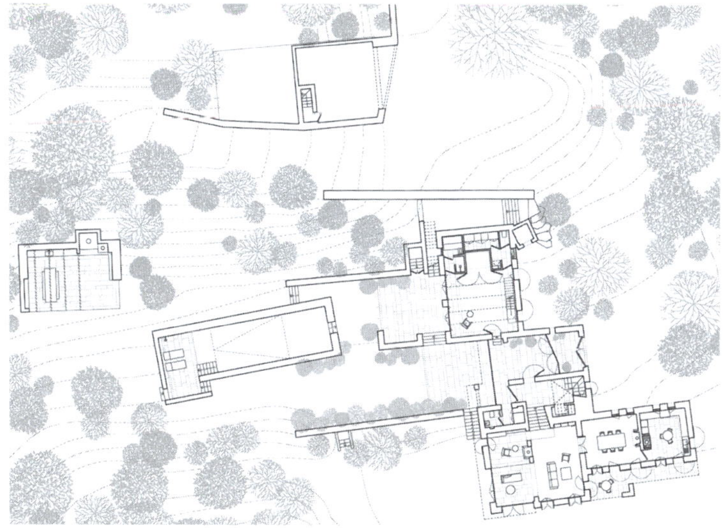

e

f

Concrete Cabin

Målselv
Norway

Completion: 2021
Area: 150 m^2
Number of Rooms: 6
Photos: André Severin Johansen

This chalet made of concrete is located on a steep slope right next to a ski resort. The house has closed fronts to the mountain and the driveway, and it is open to the panoramic landscape. The peat roof makes it look almost like an abstract extension of the landscape. The chalet was built of fiber-reinforced prefabricated concrete elements with a relief structure and assembled without joints, which gives the house a monolithic character. The bands of windows running through the façade look seamless. The interior is characterized by concrete, glass and pine. All surfaces are untreated.

Das aus Beton gebaute Chalet befindet sich an einem steilen Hang direkt neben einem Skigebiet. Das Haus ist zum Berg und zur Zufahrtsseite hin geschlossen und öffnet sich zur Aussicht. Das mit Torf bedeckte Dach lässt das Gebäude wie eine abstrakte Erweiterung der Landschaft wirken. Das Chalet wurde aus faserverstärkten, vorgefertigten Betonelementen mit Reliefstruktur konstruiert und fugenlos verbaut, was dem Haus einen monolithischen Charakter gibt. Durchgehende Fensterbänder erscheinen in der Fassade ungebrochen. Im Inneren dominieren die Materialien Beton, Glas und Kiefernholz. Alle Oberflächen sind unbehandelt.

a **Interior view dining and living area with fireplace and panoramic view.** Innenansicht Ess- und Wohnbereich mit Kamin und Panoramablick.

a

b

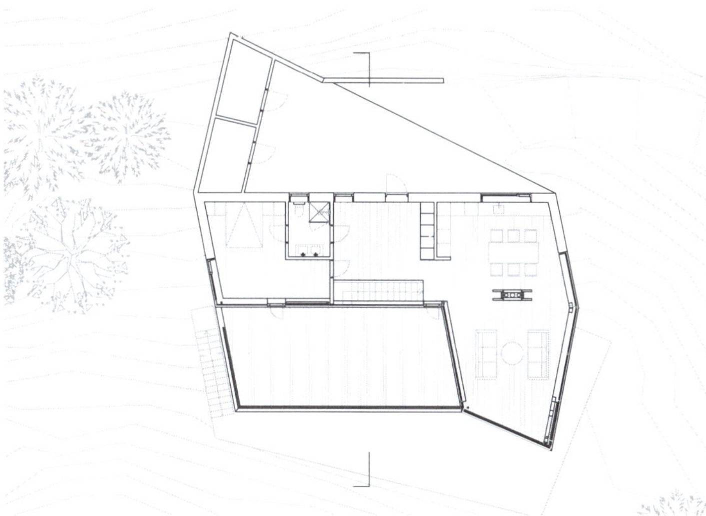

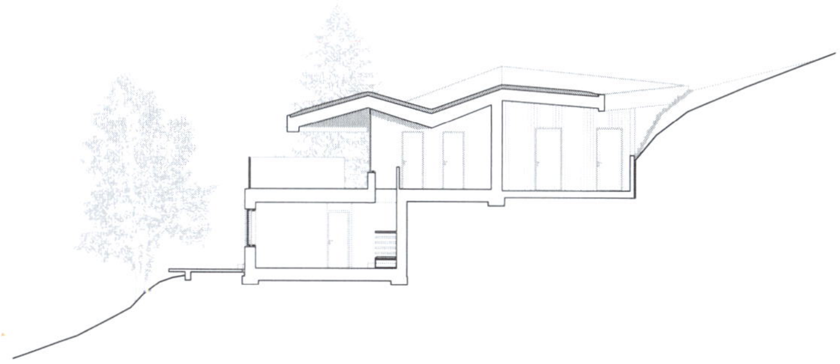

c d

b **Exterior view with snow.**
Außenansicht mit Schnee.

c **Second floor plan.**
Grundriss 1. Obergeschoss.

d **Concrete Cabin cross section.**
Querschnitt Concrete Cabin.

e **Detail of the exterior façade.**
Detail der Außenfassade.

e

Chalet La Transhumance

Saint-Martin-de-Belleville France

Completion: 2011
Area: 530 m²
Number of Rooms: 19
Photos: Vincent Leroux

The interior design of this family house, far from having the geometric structure of a traditional chalet, is a kind of homely landscape of shapes that rise from the ground like mountains from the valley. A set of lines and organic shapes, clearly flowing and modern, are composed around a wooden ribbon. A large main room on top of the entire structure is the chalet's central point, where the family gathers around an open fireplace.

Weit entfernt von der geometrischen Bauweise eines traditionellen Chalets ist die Innenarchitektur dieses Familienhauses eine häusliche Landschaft, deren Formen sich aus dem Boden erheben wie Berge aus einem Tal. Eine Komposition aus fließenden Linien und organischen Formen gruppiert sich um ein mit Holz verkleidetes Band. Ein großer Hauptraum erhebt sich über die gesamte Konstruktion und bildet den zentralen Punkt des Chalets, an dem sich die Familie um einen offenen Kamin versammelt.

a **View of the bedroom.**
Blick ins Schlafzimmer.

b **Interior view lounge.**
Innenansicht Lounge.

a b

c

d

c **Interior view of a room.**
Innenansicht eines Zimmers.

d **Entrance area.**
Eingangsbereich.

e **Section of the living area in the attic.**
Schnitt Wohnbereich im Dachgeschoss.

f **View on the private pool.**
Blick auf den privaten Pool.

e

f

Private Alpine Chalet

Austria

Completion: 2017
Area: 400 m²
Number of Rooms: 9
Photos: Christof Lackner

Just a few steps from the ski slopes, this private, modern-comfortable alpine chalet blends perfectly with the surrounding scenery. Built on a natural stone base, the chalet pays homage to the material wood by its striking timber front made of raw tree trunks. Inside, two staircases, as steep as mountain paths, connect the main and first floors. Interiors take up old familiar elements in a modern way. A large terrace overlooking the valley makes the landscape the protagonist and large window fronts on the main floor marry the breathtaking views of the mountains with the warm, cozy interior.

Das private modern-komfortable Alpenchalet, nur wenige Schritte von den Skipisten entfernt, fügt sich harmonisch in die umliegende Szenerie ein. Erbaut auf einem natürlichen Natursteinsockel, ist das Chalet mit seiner auffälligen Holzfassade aus rohen Baumstämmen eine Hommage an das Material Holz. Im Inneren verbinden zwei Treppen, steil wie Bergpfade, Haupt- und Obergeschoss. Die Innenräume greifen althergebrachte Elemente in moderner Form wieder auf. Eine große Terrasse, die sich zum Tal hin öffnet, macht die Landschaft zum Protagonisten und große Fensterfronten im Hauptgeschoss verbinden die atemberaubende Aussicht auf die Berge mit dem warmen, gemütlichen Interior.

a **Interior view "Stube" with fireplace and relaxation area.**
Innenansicht „Stube" mit Kamin und Ruhebereich.

a

b

c

b **View of the mountains from the terrace.**
Blick auf die Berge von der Terrasse.

c **Interior view dining area with large panoramic windows.**
Innenansicht Essbereich mit großen Panoramafenstern.

d **Longitudinal section.**
Längsschnitt.

e **Exterior detail of the roof structure.**
Äußeres Detail der Dachstruktur.

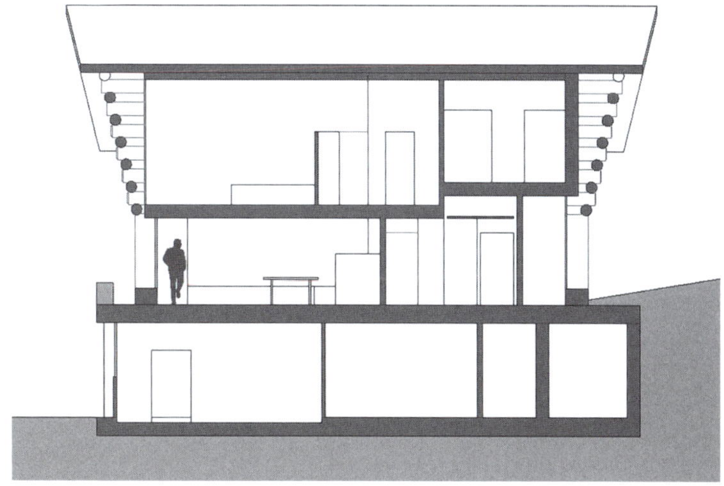

d

e

Twisted Cabin

Kvitfjell
Norway

Completion: 2011
Area: 360 m²
Number of Rooms: 5 bedrooms and 2 lofts
Photos: Nils Petter Dale and JVA

High up in the mountains, 1,000 meters above sea level and close to the ski slopes, this modern chalet reflects the contours of the terrain and can accommodate a large family. The chalet has seven floors that are connected in several ways to the surrounding terrain. All of these interlocking levels offer several exciting interior and exterior views. The façade and roof are clad in dark larch wood, while the interior of the chalet is furnished and equipped mainly with oak wood to provide comfort in winter.

Hoch in den Bergen, 1.000 Meter über dem Meer und in der Nähe der Skipisten, spiegelt das moderne Chalet die Konturen des Geländes wider und schafft Platz für eine große Familie. Das Chalet hat sieben Stockwerke, die unterschiedlich mit dem umliegenden Gelände verbunden sind. Diese verschachtelten Ebenen bieten verschiedene, interessante Innen- und Außenansichten. Die Fassade und das Dach sind mit dunklem Lärchenholz verkleidet, während das Innere des Chalets hauptsächlich in Eichenholz ausgestattet und eingerichtet ist, um im Winter für Behaglichkeit zu sorgen.

a **Interior view of the kitchen and dining area with large windows.**
Innenansicht Küche und Essbereich mit großen Fenstern.

a

b

c d

b **Exterior view from the garden.**
Außenansicht vom Garten.

c **View of the bedroom.**
Blick ins Schlafzimmer.

d **Interior view of the hallway clad in larch wood.**
Innenansicht Flur verkleidet mit Lärchenholz.

e **Twisted Cabin floor plan.**
Grundriss Twisted Cabin.

f **Exterior view at sunset.**
Außenansicht bei Sonnenuntergang.

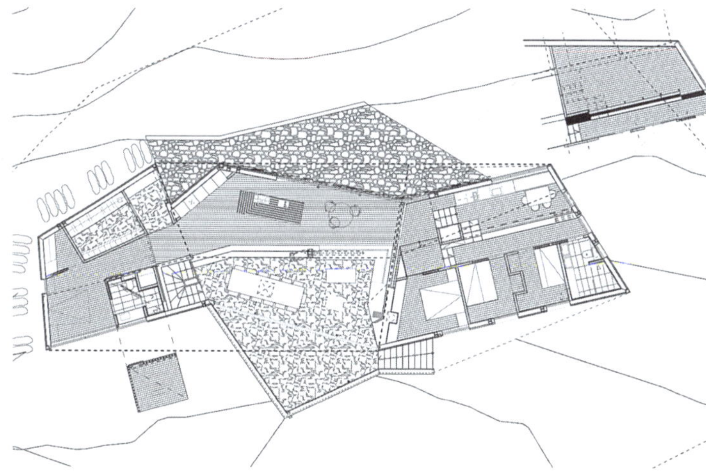

e

f

The Crow's Nest

California
USA

Completion: 2014
Area: 520 m²
Number of Rooms: 12
Photos: Bruce Damonte

This chalet is on a slope in the Sierra Nevada at an altitude of 7,300 feet above sea level. An axial concrete aisle with arched openings defines the base floor and anchors the house to the mountain. The upper floors are placed on the base of the house, similar to a nest on a tree or rocky outcrop. A three-story steel staircase framed by a large window overlooking the mountains creates a sense of vertical movement. The central living room impresses with double height, an imposing natural stone fireplace and spectacular views of nature.

Dieses Chalet befindet sich in der Sierra Nevada, am Hang gelegen auf einer Höhe von 7.300 Fuß. Das Sockelgeschoss wird durch ein axiales Betonschiff mit bogenförmigen Öffnungen definiert, welches das Haus am Berg verankert. So wie ein Nest auf einem Baum oder einem Felsvorsprung sitzt, ruhen die oberen Stockwerke des Hauses auf diesem Betonsockel. Die vertikale Bewegung durch das Haus wird durch eine dreistöckige Stahltreppe vermittelt, die von einem riesigen Fenster mit Blick auf die Berge eingerahmt wird. Das zentrale Wohnzimmer beeindruckt mit doppelter Höhe, imposantem Natursteinkamin und dem spektakulären Blick in die Natur.

a **Interior view kitchen with view of the surrounding landscape.** Innenansicht Küche mit Blick auf die umliegende Landschaft.

b **Staircase with panoramic window.** Treppenhaus mit Panoramafenster.

a b

c

d

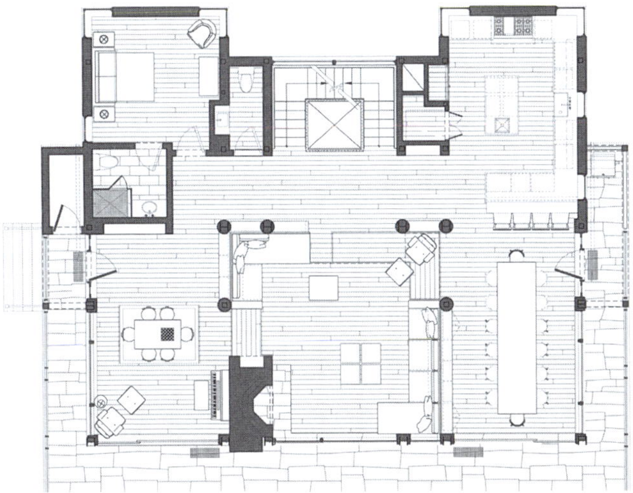

e

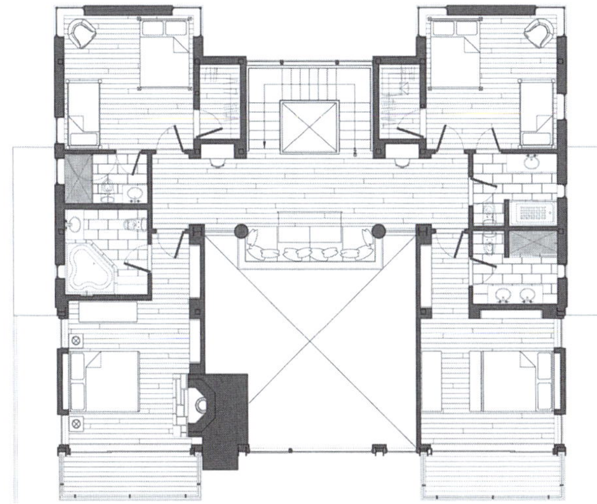

f

c Living room with large windows and fireplace.
Wohnzimmer mit großen Fenstern und Kamin.

d Exterior view of the chalet at night.
Außenansicht Chalet bei Nacht.

e Third floor plan.
Grundriss 2. Obergeschoss.

f Fourth floor plan.
Grundriss 3. Obergeschoss.

g Interior view bedroom with panoramic windows.
Innenansicht Schlafzimmer mit Panoramascheiben.

g

GlamBOX Cabin

Garessio Italy

Studio Officina82

Completion: 2021
Area: 22 m²
Number of Rooms: 1
Photos: Andrea Ferrari – Pepe Fotografia

Inspired by the haystacks and cottages of its surroundings, GlamBOX is a unique project that is in harmony with the landscape. This is a place where traditional, rural architecture is combined with innovative design to become a very special unity. A 5 x 3 m module on the first floor, made of chestnut wood, offers space for the bedroom and bathroom together with stargazing, while the attic has two additional beds for children. Whoever prefers, can move the bed right out onto the terrace!

Inspiriert von den Heuschobern und Hütten der Umgebung, ist GlamBOX ein einzigartiges Projekt, das sich harmonisch in das Landschaftsbild einfügt. Hier verbinden sich traditionelle, ländliche Architektur mit einer innovativen Gestaltung zu einer besonderen Einheit. Für die Unterbringung in Verbindung mit der Sternenbeobachtung bietet das 5 x 3 m große Modul aus Kastanienholz im Erdgeschoss Platz für das Schlaf- und Badezimmer, im Dachgeschoss stehen zwei weitere Betten für Kinder zur Verfügung. Wer möchte, kann das Bett gleich auf die Terrasse schieben!

a **Interior view of the sleeping area with mezzanine.**
Innenansicht Schlafbereich mit Mezzanin.

a

b

c

b **Interior view of the mezzanine.**
Innenansicht der Mezzanine.

c **Exterior view of the chalet amidst nature.**
Außenansicht des Chalets inmitten der Natur.

d **First floor plan.**
Grundriss Erdgeschoss.

e **GlamBOX Cabin cross section.**
Querschnitt GlamBOX Cabin.

f **View of the sliding bed on the platform.**
Blick auf das Schiebebett auf der Plattform.

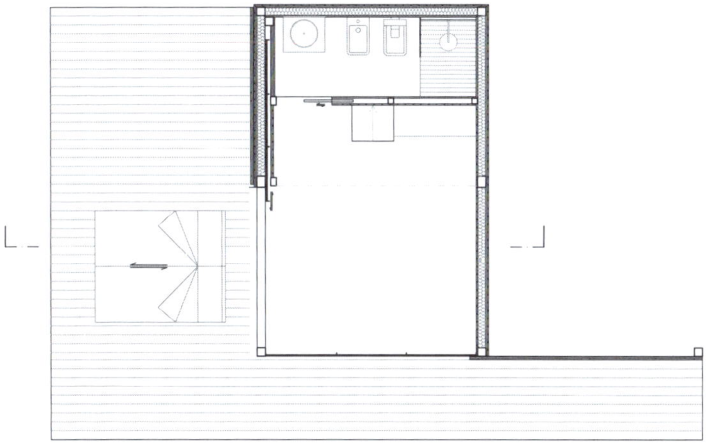

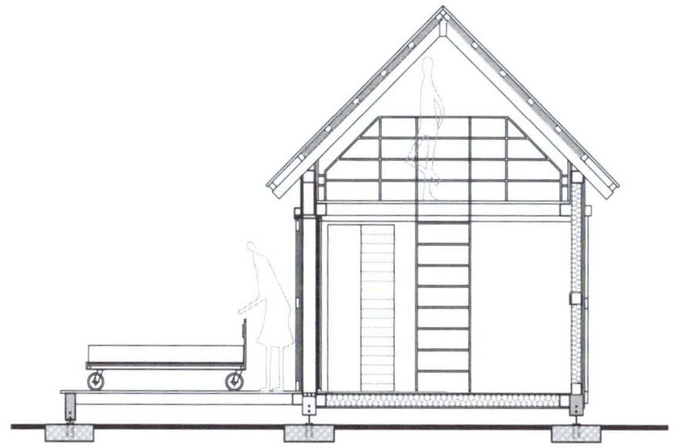

d e

f

Chalet Noisettes

Gryon
Switzerland

Completion: 2008
Area: 170 m²
Number of Rooms: 7
Photos: Joël Tettamanti and Milo Keller

The extension of a small, 100-year-old chalet on the outskirts of Gryon was approached with great sensitivity. A winter garden, which looks like an abstract miniature of the existing chalet, complements the building. On the north side, a tower was built to house the bathrooms. The two new volumes, which look as if they are floating on their pedestals, mutually reinforce their relationship with the existing building. The façades of the extensions are made of layered, untreated, heated and charred larch wood, creating a dialogue between old and new. Inside, both volumes are white, highlighting the contrast between the chalet's exterior timber and its new rooms.

Mit viel Fingerspitzengefühl wurde ein kleines, 100 Jahre altes Chalet am Rande von Gryon erweitert. Ein Wintergarten, der wie eine abstrakte Miniatur des bestehenden Chalets wirkt, ergänzt das Gebäude. Auf der Nordseite entstand ein Turm, in dem sich die Bäder befinden. Beide neuen Volumen, die auf ihren Sockeln zu schweben scheinen, verstärken gegenseitig ihre Beziehung zum Bestandsbau. Die Fassaden der Anbauten bestehen aus geschichtetem Lärchenholz, unbehandelt, erhitzt und verkohlt, wodurch ein Dialog zwischen Alt und Neu entsteht. Im Inneren sind beide Volumen weiß, was den Kontrast zwischen dem Holz des Chalets und den neuen Räumen hervorhebt.

a **Interior view of the dining and living area.**
Innenansicht Ess- und Wohnbereich.

a

b

c

b **Living area with fireplace and panoramic window.**
Wohnbereich mit Kamin und Panoramafenster.

c **Exterior view of the new extension.**
Außenansicht der neuen Erweiterung.

d **Basement floor plan.**
Grundriss Untergeschoss.

e **First floor plan.**
Grundriss Erdgeschoss.

f **Second floor plan.**
Grundriss Obergeschoss.

g **Exterior view with snow at night.**
Außenansicht mit Schnee bei Nacht.

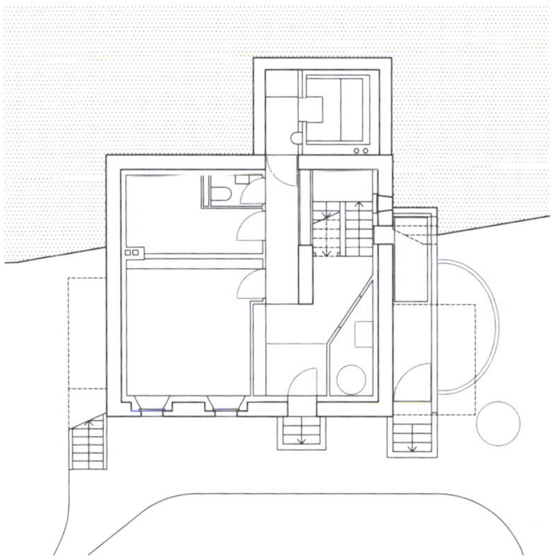

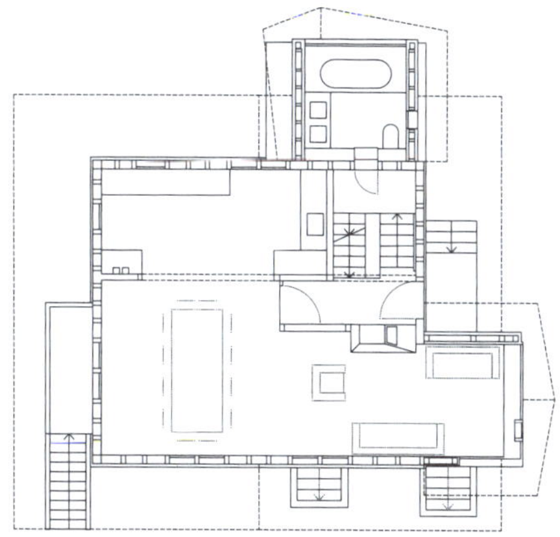

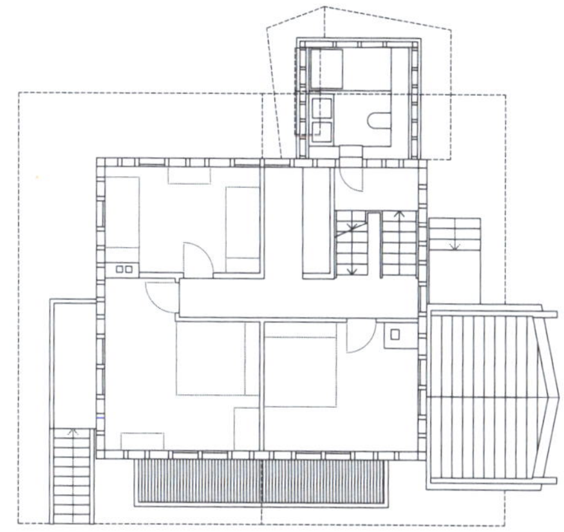

d e f

g

Mountain House

Jämtland
Sweden

Completion: 2013
Area: 111 m²
Number of Rooms: 7
Photos: Åke E:Son Lindman

The two-storey chalet is nestled in beautiful nature, right next to a ski slope in Edsåsdalen. The upper floor with its large open living, dining and kitchen has access via a footbridge. Downstairs it houses three bedrooms, two bathrooms and a sauna. The façade, interior walls and floors are made of wood, which creates a homely and warm atmosphere throughout the house. Despite the steep ground the house is built on, all rooms – even the bedroom facing the mountain – have windows on at least two sides, so that the shifting mountain light reaches every nook and cranny of the home.

Das zweigeschossige Chalet liegt eingebettet in die wunderschöne Natur, direkt an einer Skipiste in Edsåsdalen. Über einen Steg erreicht man das Obergeschoss mit seinem großen, offenen Wohn-, Ess- und Küchenbereich. Auf der unteren Ebene befinden sich drei Schlafzimmer, zwei Bäder und eine Sauna. Fassade, Innenwände und Böden sind aus Holz gestaltet und schaffen so eine wohnliche und warme Atmosphäre im gesamten Haus. Trotz des steilen Geländes, auf dem das Haus gebaut ist, haben alle Räume – sogar das zum Berg hin gelegene Schlafzimmer – auf mindestens zwei Seiten Fenster, so dass das ständig wechselnde Licht der Berge jeden Winkel des Gebäudes erreicht.

a **Living room with Danish Scan Spis fireplace.**
Wohnzimmer mit Danish Scan Spis Kamin.

b **Footbridge to the main entrance.**
Fußgängerbrücke zum Haupteingang.

a b

C

c **Exterior view south façade.**
Außenansicht Südfassade.

d **North-south section.**
Schnitt Nord-Süd.

e **Interior view of the kitchen and dining area.**
Innenansicht Küche und Essbereich.

f **Living room facing south overlooking the valley.**
Wohnzimmer nach Süden mit Blick auf das Tal.

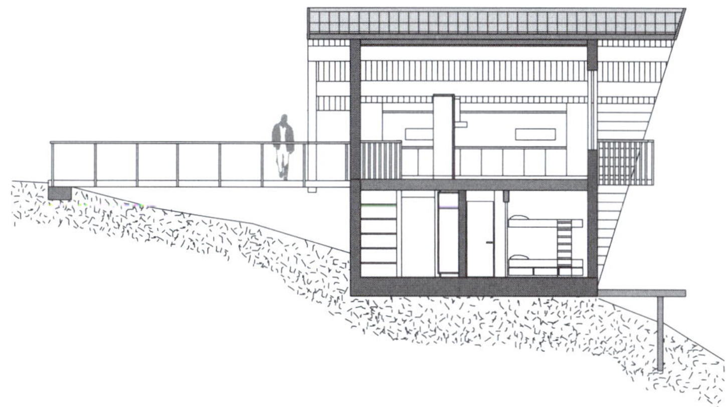

d

e f

La Baita Inhabitant a Rustic

Valle dell'Orco
Italy

Completion: 2019
Area: 70 m² + 20 m² cellar
Number of Rooms: 2
Photos: Dario Muzzarini

The little house is beautiful from the outside, as it is, and that's why it was preserved. But inside it was transformed into a comfortable and welcoming, functional house. Instead of a stable with wooden troughs, the ground floor is now a large living area with a stone vault. The first floor served as a barn and is now a comfortable sleeping area with a pitched roof. It is only a new interior staircase and a new bathroom that change the original layout . The chalet got a new basement that was built just in front of the house using stones that were unearthed during the excavations.

Von außen ist das kleine Häuschen schön, wie es ist, und wurde darum erhalten. Aber das Innere wurde in ein komfortables und einladendes, funktionelles Haus verwandelt. Anstelle eines Stalls mit Holztrögen ist nun ein großer Wohnbereich mit einem Steingewölbe im Erdgeschoss entstanden. Der erste Stock fungierte als Scheune und ist nun ein komfortabler Schlafbereich mit Dachschräge geworden. Lediglich eine neue Innentreppe und ein neues Bad verändern den ursprünglichen Raum. Ergänzt wurde das Chalet um einen neuen Keller, der vor das Haus gebaut wurde, indem die bei den Ausgrabungen zutage getretenen Felsbrocken wiederverwendet wurden.

a **View of the kitchen made of chestnut wood and a local stone slab.**
Blick in die Küche aus Kastanienholz mit lokaler Steinplatte.

a

b

c d

b Sleeping area in chestnut wood with tatami mats.
Schlafbereich aus Kastanienholz mit bündig Tatami-Matten.

c New window overlooking the existing rustic stones and the landscape.
Neues Fenster mit Blick auf die bestehenden rustikalen Steine und die Landschaft.

d New staircase made of chestnut wood.
Neue Treppe aus Kastanienholz.

e Sketch concept.
Skizze Konzept.

f Exterior view of plot.
Außenansicht vom Grundstück.

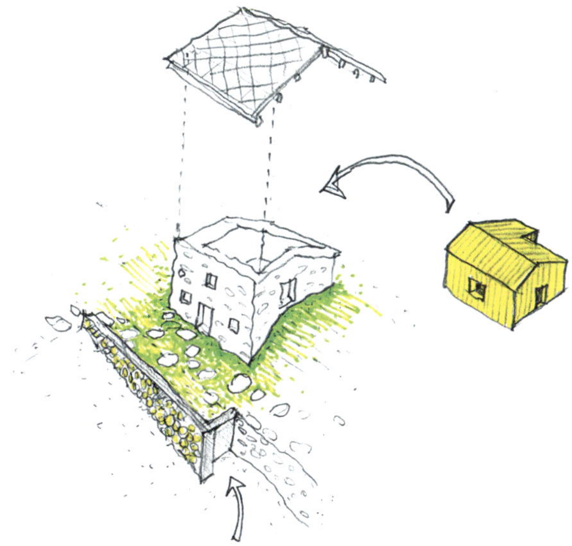

e

f

La Petite Maison

164

Nendaz Switzerland

Completion: 2021
Area: 80 m²
Number of Rooms: 3.5
Photos: Julie Masson

This small wooden house and its workshop in Haute-Nendaz are nestled in a wooded area, seemingly cut off from the rest of the world. Its concept is a simple monolith, completely covered on its five sides with larch panels, making the house merge with the surrounding vegetation. Inside, a central staircase constitutes the backbone of the house, providing access to the five half-levels, each comprising two different rooms. This kind of internal labyrinth opens a succession of "small worlds" that give the feeling of living in a place larger than it actually is.

Dieses kleine Holzhaus und die dazugehörige Werkstatt befinden sich in Haute-Nendaz und sind eingebettet in ein Waldstück, scheinbar vom Rest der Welt abgeschnitten. Der Entwurf formt einen schlichten Monolith, der an seinen fünf Seiten vollständig mit einer Verkleidung aus rauen Lärchenholzstreifen bedeckt ist, wodurch er sich in die pflanzliche Umgebung einfügt. Die fünf Halbebenen, die jeweils aus zwei unterschiedlichen Räumen bestehen, können über eine zentrale Treppe im Inneren des Hauses erschlossen werden, die das Rückgrat des Objekts bildet. Dieses innere Labyrinth eröffnet eine Abfolge von „kleinen Welten" und schafft so das Gefühl, an einem Ort zu leben, der größer wirkt, als er tatsächlich ist.

a **Interior view of the living room.**
Innenansicht Wohnzimmer.

a

b c

d

e f g

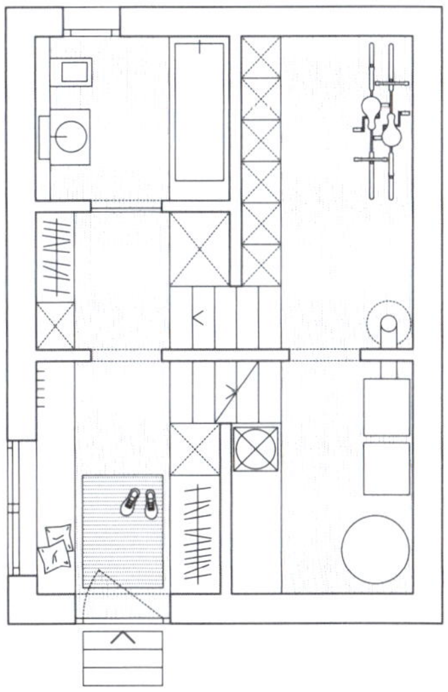

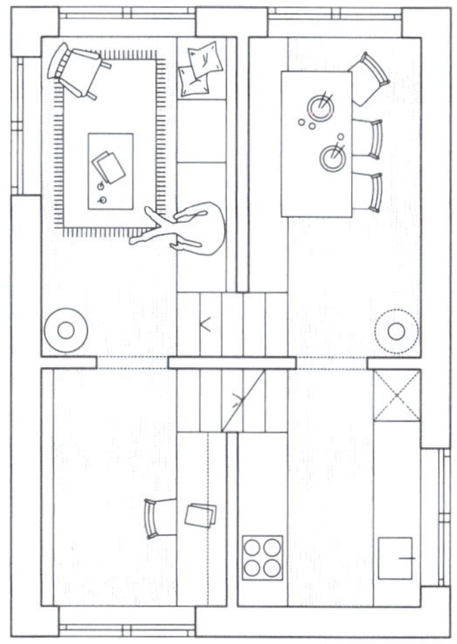

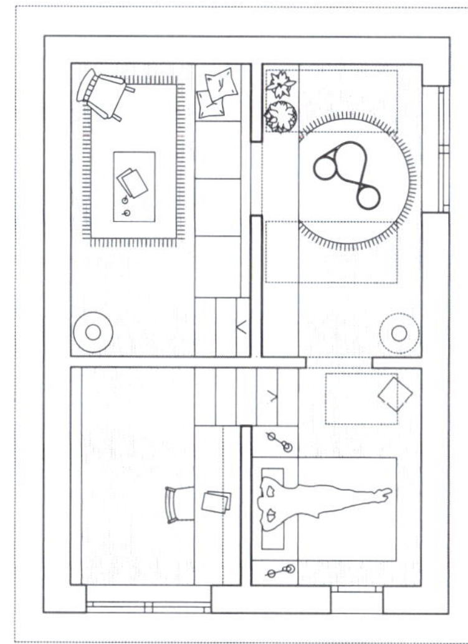

b **Interior view of the bedroom.**
Innenansicht Schlafzimmer.

c **View into the library room.**
Blick in den Bibliotheksraum.

d **Exterior view of La Petite Maison from the garden.**
Außenansicht von La Petite Maison vom Garten.

e **First floor plan.**
Grundriss Erdgeschoss.

f **Second floor plan.**
Grundriss 1. Obergeschoss.

g **Attic floor plan.**
Grundriss Dachgeschoss.

h **Façade made of local larch wood slats.**
Fassade aus Lärchenholzlamellen aus der Region.

h

Alpenchalet

Walchensee
Germany

Arnold/Werner Architektur

Completion: 2014
Area: 70 m²
Number of Rooms: 2
Photos: Kilian Bishop

In the idyllic village of Walchensee in Upper Bavaria, a house from the 70's underwent an interior transformation to become a modern and cozy alpine chalet for exquisite stays at any season of the year. The garden floor houses a guest studio with garden view. The walls are plastered with clay and painted gray. The old concrete ceiling from the 70s kept its original roughness by its small slabs. Further characteristics are a free-standing concrete kitchen, and an open fireplace clad with stones from the local mountain river. All wooden furniture was specially designed for this object and made of local wood.

Im idyllisch gelegenen Ort Walchensee in Oberbayern wurde ein Bestandshaus aus den 1970er-Jahren innenarchitektonisch in ein modernes und warmes Alpenchalet umgestaltet, das zu jeder Jahreszeit eine hohe Aufenthaltsqualität bietet. Im Gartengeschoss befindet sich ein Studio für Gäste mit freiem Blick in den Garten. Die Wände wurden mit Lehm verputzt und grau gestrichen. Die alte Betondecke aus den 1970er-Jahren wurde in Ihrer Rohheit aus kleinen Schalbrettern belassen. Weitere Ausstattungsmerkmale sind eine freie Betonküche, ein offener Kamin, welcher mit Steinen aus dem heimischen Bergfluss verschalt wurde. Sämtliche Holzmöbel wurden für dieses Objekt entworfen und aus heimischen Holz gefertigt.

a **Dining room with panoramic window.**
Esszimmer mit Panoramafenster.

b

c

b **Living room with corner sofa and fireplace.**
Wohnzimmer mit Ecksofa und Kamin.

c **Interior view of the dining and sleeping area.**
Innenansicht Ess- und Schlafbereich.

d **First floor plan.**
Grundriss Erdgeschoss.

e **Interior view of the kitchen with access to the garden.**
Innenansicht Küche mit Zugang zum Garten.

d

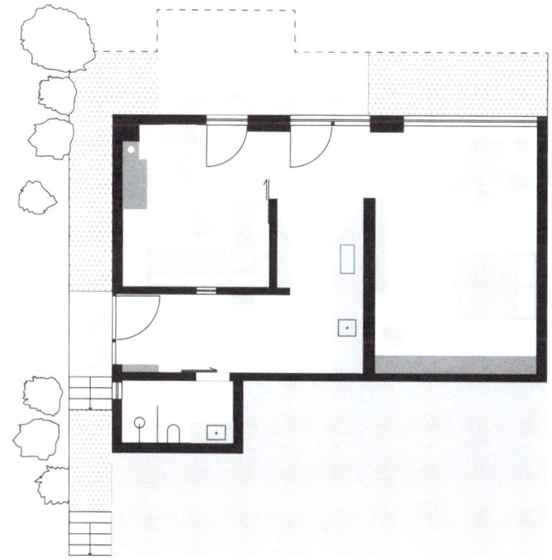

e

Baita 1697

Pragelato
Italy

Completion: 2010
Area: 450 m²
Number of Rooms: 12
Photos: Massimo Listri

In compliance with the strict Italian building laws, designed to protect and preserve the architectural heritage of the region, the house Baita 1697 was rebuilt by the owner and architect Lucie McCullough to incorporate the essentials of the original features and structures: beautiful vaulted stone ceilings on the first floor, the original ceiling in its modern kitchen and most of the original wood. On top of that, a terrace was carved into the traditional stone roof with floor-to-ceiling windows, a hot tub was installed on the terrace, and a large copper bathtub was added to one of the bedrooms.

Unter Einhaltung der strengen italienischen Baugesetze, die das architektonische Erbe der Region schützen und bewahren sollen, wurde das Haus Baita 1697 von der Eigentümerin und Architektin Lucie McCullough so umgebaut, dass es die wesentlichen ursprünglichen Merkmale und Strukturen in sich vereint: schöne gewölbte Steindecken im Erdgeschoss, die ursprüngliche Decke in der heutigen Küche und der größte Teil des ursprünglichen Holzes. Dazu kamen einige Ergänzungen wie die in das traditionelle Steindach geschnittene Terrasse mit raumhohen Fenstern, ein Whirlpool auf der Terrasse und eine große Kupferbadewanne in einem der Schlafzimmer.

a **Relaxing area opening onto a roof terrace with a hot tub.**
Entspannungsbereich mit Zugang zur Dachterrasse mit Whirlpool.

a

b

c

b **Interior view of the living room with fireplace.**
Innenansicht Wohnzimmer mit Kamin.

c **View into the kitchen.**
Blick in die Küche.

d **One of the bedrooms.**
Eines der Schlafzimmer.

e **Interior view of the dining area with vaulted stone ceilings.**
Innenansicht Essbereich mit gewölbter Steindecke.

d

e

Chalet Avantgarde

Törbel
Switzerland

Completion: 2015
Area: 110 m²
Number of Rooms: 3.5
Photos: Christian Pfammatter

In order to bring the locally prescribed chalet style up to date, the Chalet Avantgarde at an altitude of 1,800 m deliberately sets itself apart from the "heavy beam" look commonly used in roof construction. It is based on a concept of visual lightness, without visible beams, despite large roof overhangs and static requirements. The interior is characterized by the use of exclusive and explicitly contemporary knotless larch wood. It convinces with the perfect symbiosis of tranquility and yet enough variety in the wood design.

Um den lokal vorgeschriebenen Chaletstil auf das Heute zu beziehen, setzt sich das auf 1.800 m Höhe gelegene Chalet Avantgarde in der Dachkonstruktion bewusst von der häufig anzutreffenden Anmutung „schwerer Balken" ab. Der völlige Verzicht auf sichtbare Balken, trotz der großen Dachüberstände und statischen Anforderungen, unterstützt das Konzept der optischen Leichtigkeit. Der Innenausbau ist charakterisiert durch die Verwendung eines sowohl exklusiven, wie explizit modern anmutenden, astlosen Lärchenholzes. Das Überzeugende besteht in der optimalen Symbiose aus Ruhe und genügend Abwechslung im Holzmuster.

a **Interior view of the living room with panoramic windows.**
Innenansicht Wohnzimmer mit Panoramafenstern.

a

b

c

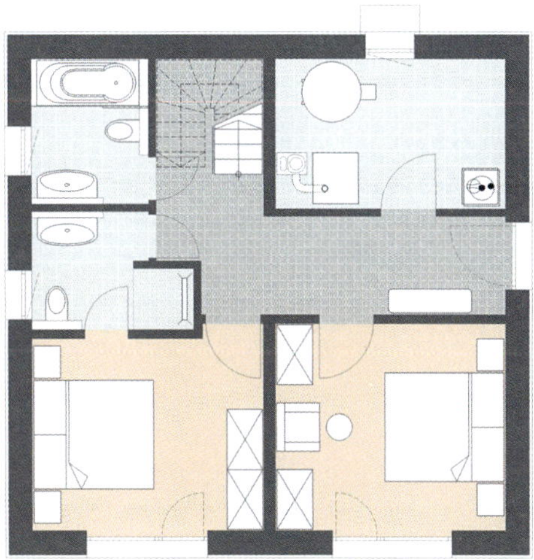

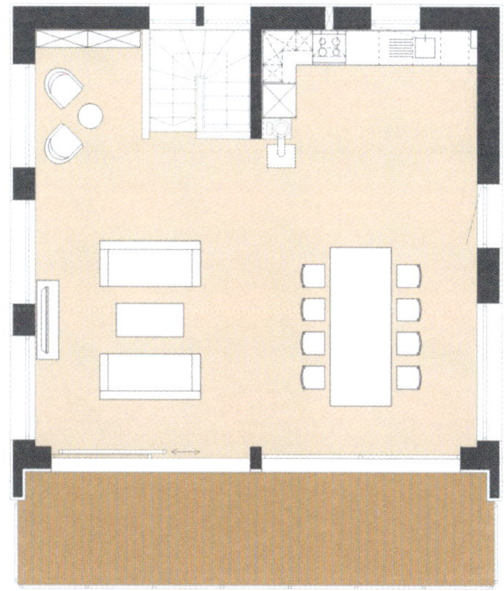

d e

b Interior view of the kitchen and living room.
Innenansicht Küche und Wohnzimmer.

c Exterior view Chalet Avantgarde from below.
Außenansicht Chalet Avantgarde von unten.

d First floor plan.
Grundriss Erdgeschoss.

e Second floor plan.
Grundriss 1. Obergeschoss.

f Interior view of a bedroom.
Innenansicht Schlafzimmer.

f

Los Cóndores Retreat

Farellones
Chile

Completion: 2018
Area: 220 m²
Number of Rooms: 7
Photos: Nico Saieh

In Farellones, a mountain village in the Andes near Santiago, a small family property was renovated and expanded. Architecture and landscaping in the neighbourhood are strongly influenced by European mountain architecture and American modernism. The pre-existing building sets the tone for the new one, which has a folded roof that relates to the topography and is open facing North to have more light (southern hemisphere). Together, these two chalets mirror the surrounding area's identity, in both material and formal terms. Thus, the ensemble built this way is in harmony with and respects the unique surroundings.

In Farellones, einem Bergdorf in den Anden in der Nähe von Santiago, wurde ein kleines Familienanwesen saniert und erweitert. Die Architektur und Landschaftsgestaltung der Umgebung sind stark von der europäischen Bergarchitektur und der amerikanischen Moderne beeinflusst. Das Bestandsgebäude ist Taktgeber für den Neubau, dessen gefaltetes Dach Bezug auf die Topographie nimmt und sich zum Nordlicht öffnet – zusammen spiegeln beide Chalets die Identität der Umgebung sowohl in materieller als auch in formaler Hinsicht wider. Das so geschaffene Ensemble fügt sich harmonisch und respektvoll in die besondere Umgebung ein.

a **Exterior detail of the Los Cóndores Retreat structure.**
Außendetail der Struktur des Los Cóndores Retreat.

a

b c

d

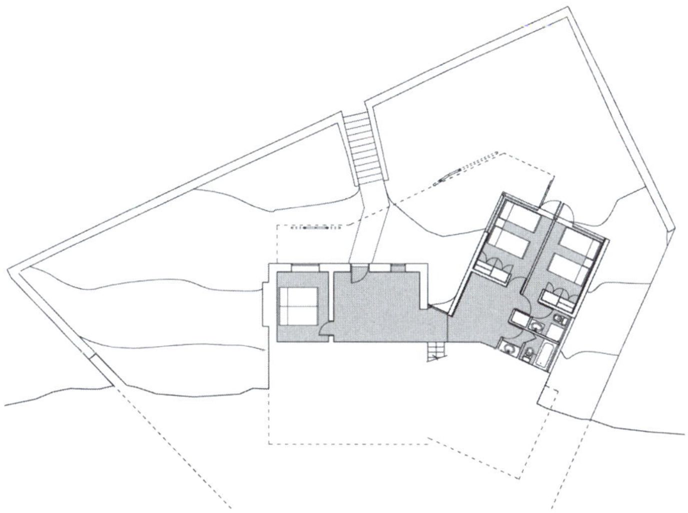

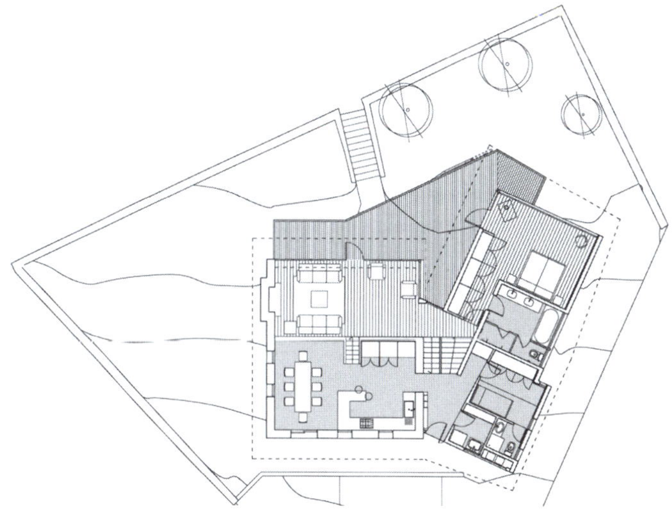

e f

b Interior view of the living area with mountain panorama.
Innenansicht Wohnbereich mit Bergpanorama.

c Side view with snow.
Seitenansicht mit Schnee.

d Los Cóndores Retreat in the mountains.
Los Cóndores Retreat in den Bergen.

e Basement floor plan.
Grundriss Untergeschoss.

f First floor plan.
Grundriss Erdgeschoss.

g Interior view of a bedroom.
Innenansicht Schlafzimmer.

g

Poisson Blanc

Québec
Canada

Completion: 2019
Area: 115 m²
Number of Rooms: 5
Photos: Raphael Thibodeau

The design concept of this is based on the site's rugged topography, steep ground on which the chalet is anchored in the rock, as well as angular and monolithic architecture. The house looks compact and minimalist due to its square plan and symmetrical gable roof, which enhances its geometric appearance. Due to budgetary limitation circulation areas were reduced and the rooms got more compact, and simple materials were used. Views of the surrounding landscape are framed by reduced but well-placed openings. The result is compelling and out-of-the-box architecture.

Das Konzept dieses Entwurfes ergibt sich aus der rauen Topografie des Standorts, einem abfallenden Gelände, auf dem das Chalet im Felsen verankert ist und einer kantigen und monolithischen Architektur. Kompakt und minimalistisch zeigt sich das Haus mit seinem quadratischen Grundriss. Das symmetrische Satteldach verstärkt das geometrische Erscheinungsbild noch. Das bescheidene Budget führte zu einer Reduzierung der Verkehrsflächen und zur Schaffung kompakter Räume sowie zur Verwendung einfacher Materialien. Reduzierte, aber gezielt gesetzte Öffnungen rahmen die Ausblicke in die umgebende Landschaft. Das Ergebnis ist eine überzeugende und ungewöhnliche Architektur.

a **Interior view of the living room.**
Innenansicht Wohnzimmer.

b **Exterior view from the surroundings.**
Außenansicht aus der Umgebung.

a

b

C

c View into the kitchen and the dining area with large window.
Blick in die Küche und den Essbereich mit großem Fenster .

d First floor plan.
Grundriss Obergeschoss.

e Side view with snow.
Seitenansicht mit Schnee.

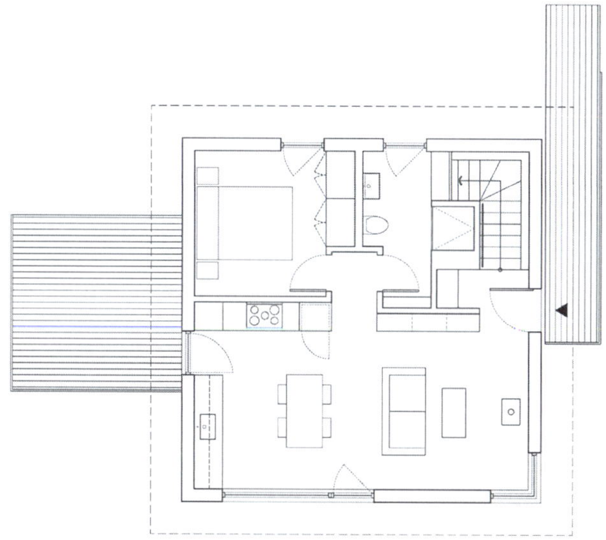

d

e

Les Préalpes A Former Guesthouse

Switzerland

Completion: 2021
Area: 150 m²
Number of Rooms: 11
Photos: Charly Jolliet

The former guest house Les Préalpes in the immediate vicinity of the famous sanatorium Le Rosaire in the Gruyère Valley was converted into three apartments and a Health-Care Center. The building's use is in relation to its original social identity. Several interventions, such as the relocation of the staircase and a new dormer in the attic, were necessary to bring some sense of unity and integrity back to the building. The design of the façades and windows echo the former rhythm and craftsman details of 1925. The main façade preserves the former entrance and its stone staircase reminding the historic past of the building.

Das ehemalige Gästehaus Les Préalpes befindet sich in unmittelbarer Nähe des berühmten Sanatoriums Le Rosaire im Greyerzer Tal und wurde nun in drei Wohnungen und ein Health-Care Center umgewandelt. Die Nutzung nimmt Bezug auf die ursprüngliche, soziale Identität des Gebäudes. Eine Vielzahl von Eingriffen, wie das Verlegen der Treppe und eine neue Gaube im Dachgeschoss waren notwendig, um dem Gebäude ein Gefühl der Ganzheitlichkeit und Integrität zurückzugeben. Die Gestaltung der Fassaden und Fenster greifen den einstigen Rhythmus und die handwerklichen Details von 1925 auf. An der Hauptfassade wurde der ehemalige Eingang mit seiner Steintreppe als historisches Zitat erhalten.

a **Interior view of the renovated roof space.**
Innenansicht des renovierten Dachgeschosses.

a

b c

d e

b Details and ornaments of the balcony.
Details und Ornamente des Balkons.

c View into the kitchen area.
Blick in den Küchenbereich.

d Chalet interior view.
Innenansicht Chalet.

e West entrance and façade.
Westeingang und Fassade.

f Cross section.
Querschnitt.

g Exterior view of the new addition.
Außenansicht des neuen Anbaus.

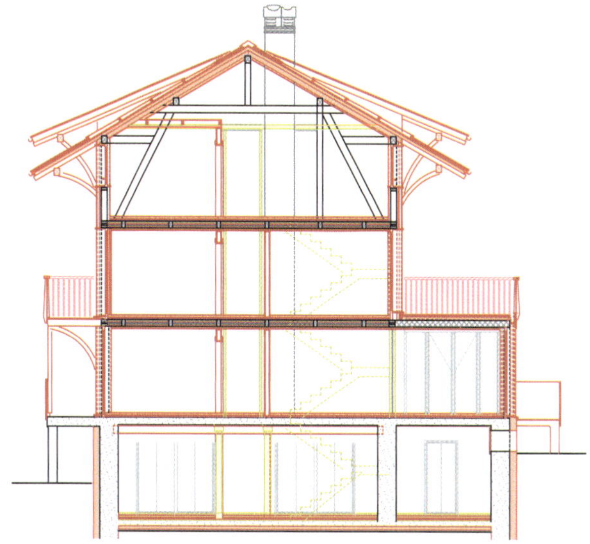

f

g

Alpine Holiday Home

Canterbury New Zealand

Completion: 2020
Area: 230 m²
Number of Rooms: 6
Photos: Anthony Turnham

Nestled amid nature and homes, in a small alpine community of Castle Hill, this cottage was designed to blend with its surroundings. It is both a retreat for a young family and a home for relatives and friends. The carefully designed wooden structure gives the house a rhythm that organizes the ample volume. The windows are placed to offer beautiful panoramic views of the mountain landscape. The East and West courtyards open to the mountains and allow one to enjoy wonderful sunrises and sunsets.

Eingebettet zwischen Natur und Häusern, in der kleinen Alpengemeinde Castle Hill, wurde dieses Ferienhaus so konzipiert, dass es mit seiner Umgebung verschmilzt. Es ist gleichzeitig Rückzugsort für eine junge Familie und Gastgeber für Verwandte und Freunde. Die sorgfältig konstruierte Holzstruktur gibt dem Haus einen Rhythmus, der das großzügige Volumen gliedert. Gut gesetzte Verglasungen geben wundervolle und weite Ausblicke auf die Bergkulisse frei. Von den Ost- und Westhöfen, die sich zur Bergwelt öffnen, lassen sich die herrlichen Sonnenauf und -Untergänge geniessen.

a **Interior view of the living room with panoramic window.**
Innenansicht Wohnzimmer mit Panoramafenster.

a

b

c d

b Interior view of the dining and living area with bench.
Innenansicht Ess- und Wohnbereich mit Sitzbank.

c **Bathroom on the second floor.**
Badezimmer im ersten Obergeschoss.

d **Interior view of the bedroom with bunk beds.**
Innenansicht Schlafzimmer mit Kojenbetten.

e **First floor plan.**
Grundriss Erdgeschoss.

f **West exterior view at twilight.**
Westliche Außenansicht in der Abenddämmerung.

e

f

Mountain House

Manigod France

Completion: 2016
Area: 200 m²
Number of Rooms: 6
Photos: Olivier-Martin Gambier and Simone Bossi

The Mountain House complies with all local strict architectural constraints, avoiding all artificial or superfluous elements. The building is a typical stack house and was designed in layers according to the program: parking, machine room and ski storage on the ground floor. Bedrooms on the first floor and living area on the top floor. Moving from more dark, compact spaces to gradually more open, luminous spaces with higher ceiling and greater vistas. Its base is of poured exposed concrete, while the upper floors are of wood. To make the concept tangible, the selection of materials is limited.

Das Mountain House erfüllt alle vor Ort geltenden, strengen architektonischen Auflagen und vermeidet dabei alle künstlichen oder überflüssigen Elemente. Das Gebäude ist ein typisches Stapelgebäude und wurde in programmatischen Schichten konzipiert: Parkplatz, Maschinenraum und Skilager im Erdgeschoss. Schlafzimmer im Stockwerk darüber und Wohnräume im obersten Geschoss. Von dunkleren, komprimierten Räumen zu allmählich offeneren, lichtdurchfluteten Räumen mit größerer lichter Höhe und größeren Ausblicken. Der Sockel besteht aus gegossenem Sichtbeton, die darüber liegenden Etagen aus Holz. Für die Erlebbarkeit des Konzeptes fiel die Auswahl auf wenig unterschiedliche Materialien.

a **View into the living room with large window.**
Blick ins Wohnzimmer mit großem Fenster.

a

b

c

d

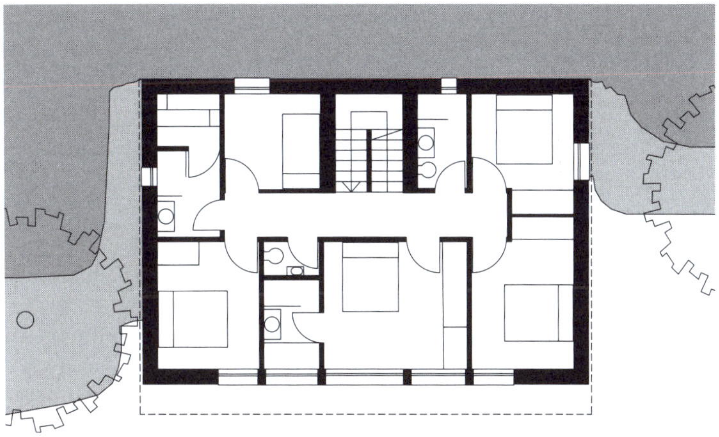

e

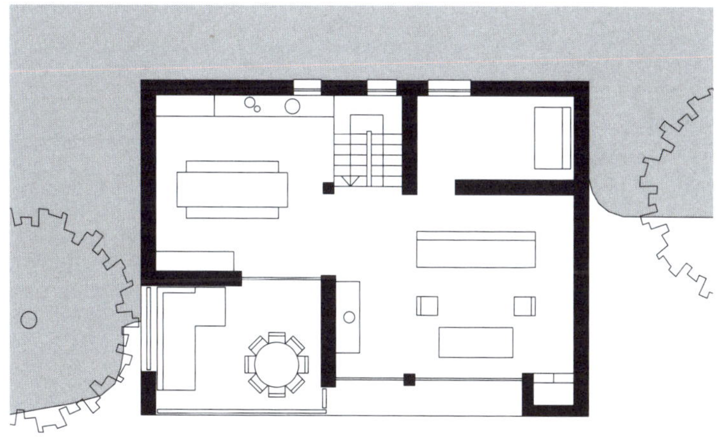

b **Living area with panoramic view and fireplace.**
Wohnbereich mit Panoramablick und Kamin.

c **Interior view of a bedroom.**
Innenansicht Schlafzimmer.

d **Second floor plan.**
Grundriss 1. Obergeschoss.

e **Attic floor plan.**
Grundriss Dachgeschoss.

f **Side view Mountain House with snow.**
Seitenansicht Mountain House mit Schnee.

f

Chalet Blanc

Breuil-Cervinia Italy

Completion: 2020
Area: 889 m²
Number of Rooms: 5
Photos: Simone Bossi

Chalet Blanc's volume is characterized by a double roof, a tribute to the skyline of the majestic peaks at the edge of the valley. The façades are designed in different ways depending on their orientation and function. Large windows open to the south on the first floor. All rooms have access to the terraces, which are built in a zigzag pattern. Facing the harsh northwest weather, the façades are considerably much more closed, and have no large openings or protrusions. The building's prefabricated wooden structure is supported by a base clad in dry-stone masonry. The interior is characterized by original materials such as wood, stone and iron.

Das Volumen des Chalet Blanc ist durch ein Doppeldach gekennzeichnet, eine Hommage an die Skyline der majestätischen Gipfel am Rande des Tals. Die Fassaden sind je nach Ausrichtung und Funktion unterschiedlich gestaltet. Zum Süden öffnen sich große Fenster im Obergeschoss. Alle Zimmer haben Zugang zu den Terrassen, die im Zickzackmuster angelegt sind. Zum rauen Klima nach Nordwesten hin sind die Fassaden deutlich geschlossener, ohne große Öffnungen und Vorsprünge. Die vorgefertigte Holzstruktur des Gebäudes ruht auf einem gemauerten mit Trockenmauerwerk verkleideten Sockel. Ursprüngliche Materialien wie Holz, Stein und Eisen bestimmen das Interieur.

a **View from the garden to the mountains.**
Blick vom Garten auf die Berge.

a

b c

d e

b **Chalet Blanc side view.**
Seitenblick Chalet Blanc.

c **Detail of the fireplace in the living room.**
Detail Kamin im Wohnzimmer.

d **Interior view of the covered balcony.**
Innenansicht des überdachten Balkons.

e **View of a room lined completely with wood.**
Blick in einen mit Holz vollständig verkleideten Raum.

f **Side view.**
Seitenansicht.

g **Exterior view of the chalet in midst of the mountains.**
Außenansicht des Chalets inmitten der Berge.

f

g

Villa Timmerman

Gothenburg Sweden

Completion: 2020
Area: 358 m^2
Number of Rooms: 9
Photos: Kalle Sanner

On a southwest-facing slope on the west coast of Sweden stands Villa Timmerman, a semi-detached house whose two parts have a very independent appearance. They are in close correlation with the landscape and benefit from open spaces and natural light running through them. Moreover, the house's layout allows both parts to have sun light in the morning, at noon and in the evening. The dark façade of the timber house has three grids of diagonal and vertical ribs. This lattice protects against both sunlight and driving rain on the west coast. The design of the floor plan and the arrangement of the openings is based on light flux running through this structure.

An einem nach Südwesten ausgerichteten Hang an der Westküste Schwedens steht Villa Timmerman, ein Doppelhaus, dessen zwei Teile sehr eigenständig wirken. Sie stehen in enger Beziehung zur Landschaft und verfügen über fließendes Licht und offene Räume. Der Grundriss erlaubt es, dass beide Teile des Hauses Morgen-, Mittags- und Abendsonne erhalten. Auf der dunklen Fassade des Holzhauses befinden sich drei Raster aus diagonalen und vertikalen Rippen. Dieses Gitter fungiert als Schutz gegen Sonneneinstrahlung sowie gegen Treibregen an der Westküste. Der Lichtfluss durch diese Struktur bestimmt die Gestaltung des Grundrisses und die Anordnung der Öffnungen.

a **Exterior view from the garden.** Außenansicht vom Garten.

b **View from the living room to the staircase with the gallery.** Blick vom Wohnzimmer auf das Treppenhaus mit Galerie.

a b

C

c **Exterior view with snow.**
Außenansicht mit Schnee.

d **Villa Timmerman cross section.**
Querschnitt Villa Timmerman.

e **Interior view of the kitchen with peninsula.**
Innenansicht Küche mit Halbinsel.

f **Detail of the staircase window.**
Detail des Treppenhausfensters.

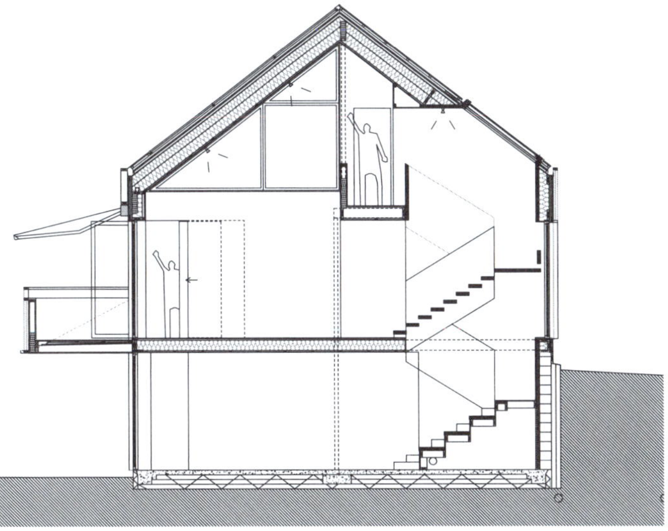

d

e f

Turmhaus Tirol

Zell am Ziller
Austria

Completion: 2018
Area: 400 m²
Number of Rooms: 5
Photos: Oliver Jaist

Turmhaus Tirol is a joint project by Grünecker Reichelt and Holzrausch. The building is based on regional construction methods and picks up characteristic features of the surrounding farmhouses and reinterprets them, such as the arrangement of windows according to their function in space, the gable roof, and the sunbaked façade. With a footprint of 8 x 8 meters, the chalet extends over six levels of the building. Three buried underground levels constitute its foundation. On top of that, another three floors of living, dining, and sleeping areas are built in wood and open stunning views of the picturesque surroundings.

Das Turmhaus Tirol ist ein gemeinsames Projekt von Grünecker Reichelt und Holzrausch. Das Gebäude orientiert sich an der regionalen Bauart und nimmt charakteristische Merkmale der umliegenden Höfe wie Anordnung der Fenster nach räumlicher Funktion, Satteldach und sonnenverbrannte Fassade auf und interpretiert diese neu. Das Chalet erstreckt sich bei einer Grundfläche von 8 x 8 Metern über sechs Gebäudeebenen. Die drei eingegrabenen Untergeschosse bilden das Fundament. Darüber erstrecken sich drei weitere Geschosse mit Wohn-, Ess- und Schlafbereichen in Holzbauweise und mit einer herrlichen Aussicht auf die malerische Umgebung.

a **Interior view of the living and dining area with panoramic window.** Innenansicht Wohn- und Essbereich mit Panoramafenster.

a

b

c

b **Attic bedroom.**
Schlafzimmer im Dachgeschoss.

c **Interior view of the living area with fireplace.**
Innenansicht Wohnecke mit Kamin.

d **Longitudinal section.**
Längsschnitt.

e **Interior details of the chalet.**
Details der Innenausstattung des Chalets.

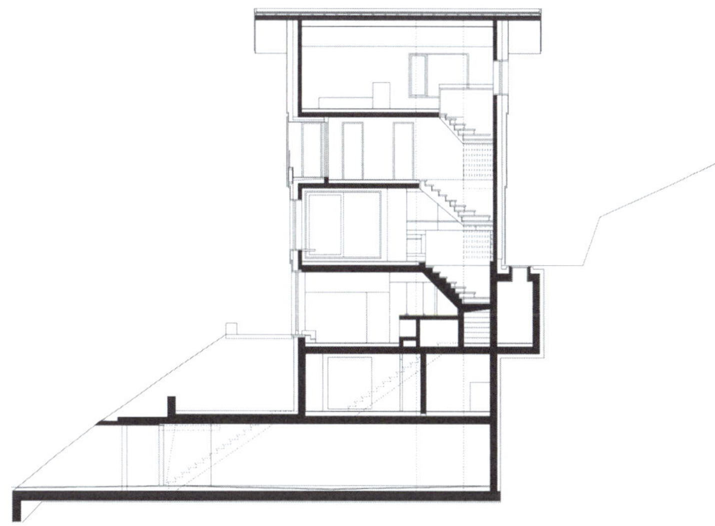

d

e

Casa Sur Ual

Vella
Switzerland

Completion: 2014
Area: 225 m²
Number of Rooms: 10
Photos: CMA and
Susanna von Känel

Surrounded by stone houses and charming timber houses, the 350-year-old house in rope structure is hardly noticeable. Demands for living space and contemporary comfort were innovatively reconciled with the historic structure through the conversion. Both owners own one third of the house and share the remaining third. The two apartments can be connected internally and can accommodate up to 15 people. The result looks like a 3D puzzle. Sometimes a corridor is 60 centimeters wide, sometimes 1.60 meters high. But comfort, quality awareness and respect for the tried and tested always prevail.

Umgeben von Steinhäusern und gefälligen Holzhäusern erweckt der 350 Jahre alte Strickbau kaum Aufsehen. Mit dem Umbau sind die Ansprüche an Wohnfläche und zeitgenössischen Komfort auf innovative Weise mit der historischen Bausubstanz in Einklang gebracht worden. Beide Eigentümer besitzen je ein Drittel des Hauses und teilen sich das restliche Drittel. Die beiden Wohnungen können intern miteinander verbundene werden und bieten so bis zu 15 Personen Platz. Das Resultat gleicht einem Puzzle im 3D-Format. Ein Durchgang ist mal 60 Zentimeter breit, ein anderer 1,60 Meter hoch. Immer aber herrscht Behaglichkeit, Qualitätsbewusstsein und der Respekt vor Altbewährtem.

a **The historic wood structure's dining and living area.**
Ess- und Wohnbereich im historischen Holzbau.

a

b c

d e

b **Reading corner with window overlooking the village.**
Leseecke mit Fenster zum Dorf.

c **View into the sleeping bunk.**
Blick in die Schlafkoje.

d **Children's room with stacked beds.**
Kinderzimmer mit gestappelten Betten.

e **Interior view of the bathroom.**
Innenansicht Badezimmer.

f **Casa Sur Ual Cross section.**
Querschnitt Casa Sur Ual.

g **Concrete staircase to the first floor with built-in wardrobe in wood.**
Betontreppe mit integriertem Holzschrank ins Obergeschoss.

f

g

Cabine A

Québec
Canada

Completion: 2019
Area: 230 m²
Number of Rooms: 6
Photos: Maxime Brouillet

The extraordinary chalet is located on a steep plot overlooking the nearby St. Lawrence River. When looking for a source of inspiration, the team of architects and graphic designers approached the International Code of Signals (ICS), which has a history of use in nautical communications. While the Alfa sign defines the overall geometry of the chalet, the entire building features subtle references to naval architecture. Cabin A's triangular roof resembles sails facing the wind, while a large wooden terrace looks like the upper deck of a ship, offering a stunning view of the river.

Das ungewöhnliche Chalet befindet sich auf einem steilen Gelände mit Blick auf den nahe gelegenen Sankt-Lorenz-Strom. Auf der Suche nach einer Inspirationsquelle wandte sich das aus Architekten und Grafikern bestehende Team dem Internationalen Signalcode (ICS) zu, der seit langem in der nautischen Kommunikation verwendet wird. Während das Alfa-Zeichen die Gesamtgeometrie des Chalets bestimmt, wurden im gesamten Gebäude subtile Bezüge zur Schiffsarchitektur hergestellt. Das dreieckige Dach von Cabine A erinnert an Segel, die sich dem Wind entgegenstellen, während eine große Holzterrasse wie das Oberdeck eines Schiffes anmutet, von dem aus man einen herrlichen Blick auf den Fluss hat.

a **Interior view of the living area with wooden corner bench and fireplace.**
Innenansicht des Wohnbereichs mit Holzeckbank und Kamin.

a

b c

d

b **View into the kitchen and dining area.**
Blick in den Küchen- und Essbereich.

c **Interior view from the staircase.**
Innenansicht vom Treppenhaus.

d **Exterior view of Cabine A with snow.**
Außenansicht Cabine A mit Schnee.

e **Cross section.**
Querschnitt.

f **Interior view of the bedroom with bunk beds.**
Innenansicht Schlafzimmer mit Kojenbetten.

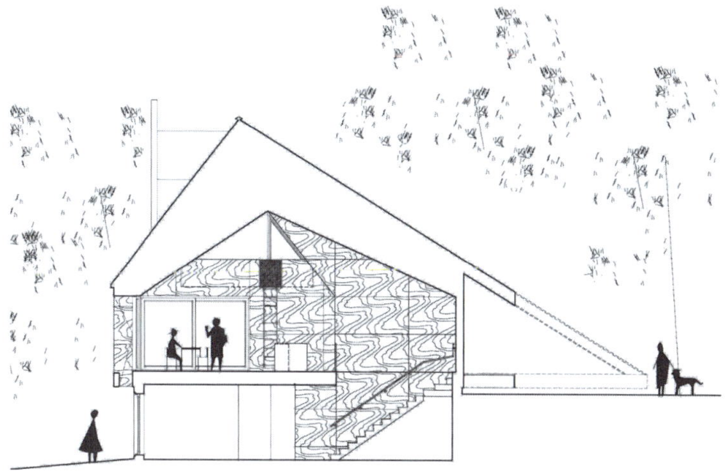

e

f

Boisset House

Orsieres Switzerland

Completion: 2012
Area: 48 m²
Number of Rooms: 4
Photos: Thomas Jantscher

Built on the hillside, the chalet offers a beautiful, unobstructed view of the Alps and the villages further down. The stone base of Boisset House was built over with a traditional log cabin construction. The living area extends over three levels on 16 square meters each and are limited by the walls of the original building. The basement was extended to accommodate the building services. Only a few interventions were made in the outer skin, such as large-scale glazing within the masonry. Thus, the view of nature staged that way is breathtakingly beautiful and creates a magical space inside.

Das am Hang gebaute Chalet bietet eine wunderschöne, freie Sicht auf die Alpen und die weiter unten gelegenen Dörfer. Der Steinsockel des Boisset House wurde mit einer traditionellen Blockhauskonstruktion überbaut. Auf je 16 qm erstreckt sich auf drei Ebenen der Wohnbereich, begrenzt durch die Bestandswände des ursprünglichen Gebäudes. Eine Erweiterung im Untergeschoss wurde für die Unterbringung der Haustechnik umgesetzt. In die äußere Hülle wurden nur wenig Eingriffe vorgenommen, wie zum Beispiel die großflächige Verglasung im Mauerwerk. Der so inszenierte Blick in die Natur ist atemberaubend schön und schafft einen magischen Raum im Inneren.

a **Interior view of the dining area with panoramic mountain views.** Innenansicht Essbereich mit Bergpanorama.

a

b

c

b **View into the bedroom with long horizontal window.**
Blick ins Schlafzimmer mit langem horizontalem Fenster.

c **Boisset House from outside with snow.**
Boisset House von außen mit Schnee.

d **Cross section.**
Querschnitt.

e **Bedroom with bunk beds.**
Schlafzimmer mit Kojenbetten.

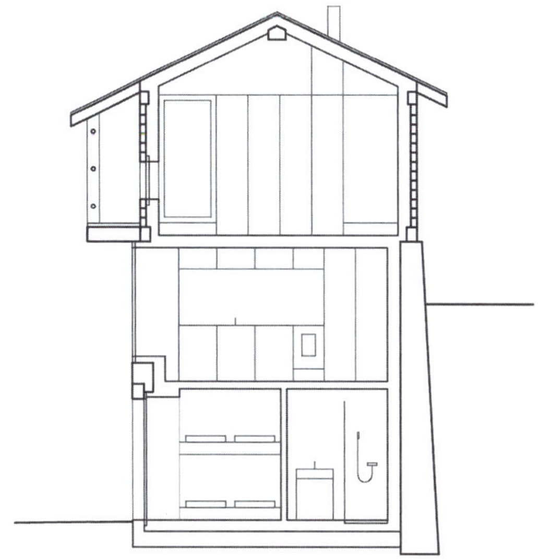

d

e

Chalet La Petite Soeur

Québec Canada

Completion: 2018
Area: 130 m²
Number of Rooms: 8
Photos: Adrien Williams

The chalet La Petite Soeur owners needed more space for their large family. Thus, an extension was built to incorporate the volumes of the existing house and, at the same time, give it the respect it deserves. The new part of the ensemble is a gentle homage to the historic house and the unique landscape in which it is nestled. The new space comes in the shape of an immaculate prism that stands on a concrete base. Its tin roof and white wood paneling are inspired by the sleek, glossy bark of birch trees that grow on the property, yet also evoke the whitewashed walls of barns in the countryside.

Die Besitzer des Chalets La Petite Soeur brauchten mehr Platz für ihre große Familie. So wurde ein Anbau geschaffen, der die Volumina des bestehenden Hauses aufnimmt und ihm gleichzeitig den nötigen Respekt erweist. Der neue Teil des Ensembles ist eine zarte Hommage an das historische Haus und die einzigartige Landschaft, in die es eingebettet ist. Der neue Raum präsentiert sich in Form eines makellosen Prismas, das auf einem Betonsockel steht. Das Blechdach und die weiße Holzverkleidung des Anbaus sind von der glatten, glänzenden Rinde der Birken inspiriert, die auf dem Grundstück wachsen, und erinnern gleichzeitig an die weiß gekalkten Wände der Scheunen auf dem Land.

a **Interior view of the dining area and new passage.**
Innenansicht Essbereich und neuer Durchgang.

a

b

c d

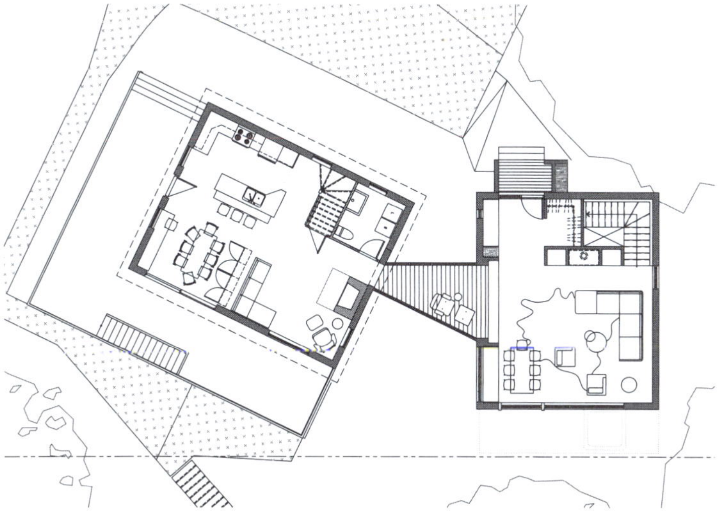

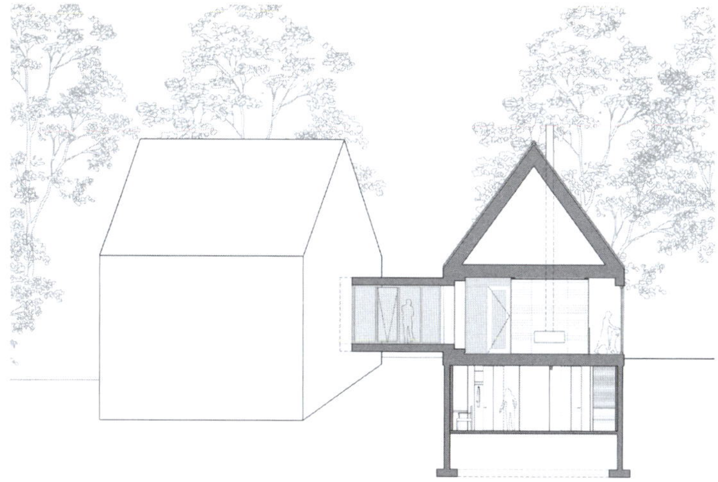

e f

b Exterior view of Chalet La Petite Soeur with snow.
Außenansicht Chalet La Petite Soeur mit Schnee.

c Interior view of the bathroom.
Innenansicht Badezimmer.

d View of the wooden stairs.
Blick auf die Holztreppe.

e First floor plan.
Grundriss Erdgeschoss.

f Cross section.
Querschnitt.

g Exterior view from below.
Außenansicht von unten.

g

Urfeld 26

228

Walchensee
Germany

Completion: 2022
Area: 80 m²
Number of Rooms: 3
Photos: Kilian Bishop

The forest landscape in Urfeld am Walchensee constitutes the setting of the restructured vacation home from the 1960s. The focus is on the intention to use existing and local resources. Thus, its skin as well as the built-in furniture were designed exclusively from silver fir from the nearby Jachenau. Inside, the focus on a small number of natural materials in conjunction with a restrained color scheme creates a room atmosphere that gives a sense of security. Thanks to photovoltaic panels integrated into the roof and the heating fireplace, the house is perfectly self-sufficient and can thus be enjoyed in the summer as well as in the winter.

Die Waldlandschaft in Urfeld am Walchensee bildet den Hintergrund für das neu strukturierte Ferienhaus aus den 1960er-Jahren. Im Mittelpunkt steht die Idee, vorhandene und lokale Ressourcen einzusetzen. So wurden die Gebäudehülle sowie die Einbaumöbel ausschließlich aus Weißtanne der nahegelegenen Gemeinde Jachenau gestaltet. Im Inneren sorgt die Konzentration auf wenige und natürliche Materialien im Zusammenhang mit einer zurückhaltenden Farbigkeit für eine Raumatmosphäre, die viel Geborgenheit ausstrahlt. Dank der dachintegrierten Photovoltaikpaneele und des Heizkamins lässt sich das Haus – sommers wie winters – wunderbar autark nutzen.

a **Relaxation area with panoramic skylight.** Entspannungsbereich mit Panoramadachfenster.

a

b

c d

b **Interior view of the dining and living area with balcony.**
Innenansicht Ess- und Wohnbereich mit Balkon.

c **Bathroom.**
Badezimmer.

d **View of the kitchen with skylight.**
Blick in die Küche mit Oberlicht.

e **First floor plan.**
Grundriss Erdgeschoss.

f **Roof detail.**
Dachdetail.

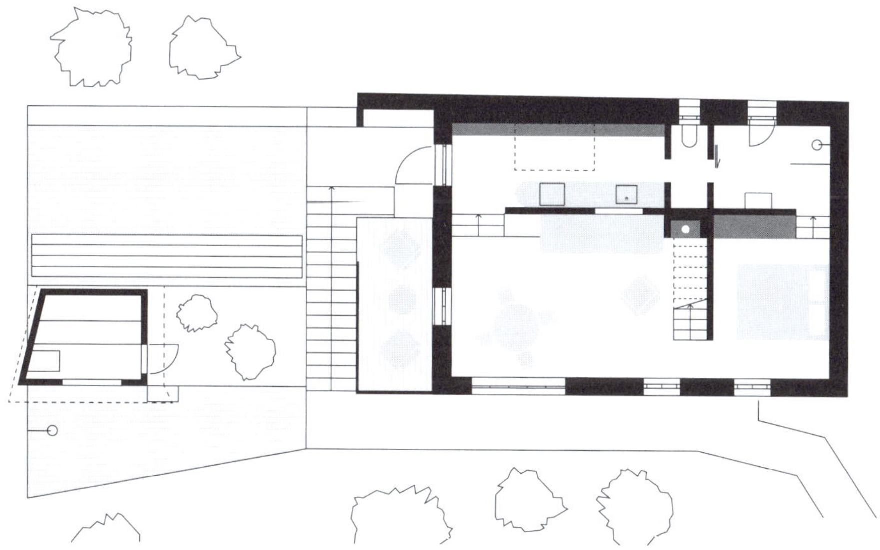

e

f

Pro-tò-ti-po 1:1 Variation of Repetition

Valtournenche Italy

Completion: 2019
Area: 35 m²
Number of Rooms: 3
Photos: Marcello Mariana
In collaboration with:
Daniele Bonetti

The chalet built in wood construction has inside and outside all the elements of a typical house. It has a living/dining room, bedroom, bathroom, and attic. It is possible to accommodate four people in this small space. The façades are made of two superimposed layers. This double structure is emphasized using different elements, materials, shades, and textures. The material contrast works perfectly: the reflection of the surfaces and the mix of the outdoor colours green, white and blue generate different moods and conditions to perceive the landscape.

Das in Holzbautechnik errichtete Chalet verfügt innen wie außen über alle typischen Elemente eines klassischen Hauses. Innen befinden sich Wohn-/Esszimmer, Schlafzimmer, Bad und Dachboden. Auf kleinem Raum können hier vier Personen untergebracht werden. Die Fassaden sind aus zwei sich überlagernden Schichten aufgebaut. Diese doppelte Struktur wird durch die Verwendung unterschiedlicher Elemente, Materialien, Farben und Texturen betont. Der Materialkontrast funktioniert perfekt: Die Reflexion der Oberflächen und die Mischung der Außenfarben grün, weiß und blau erzeugen unterschiedliche Atmosphären und Wahrnehmungen der gesamten Landschaft.

α **Exterior view of the chalet's upper level with diagonal timber elements.**
Außenansicht des oberen Teils des Chalets mit diagonalen Holzelementen.

α

b

c

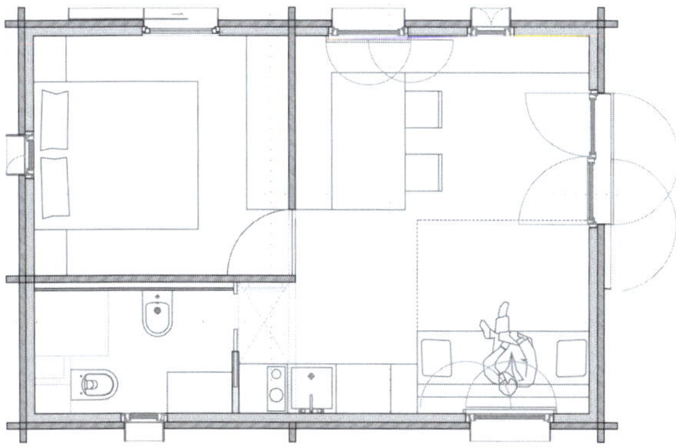

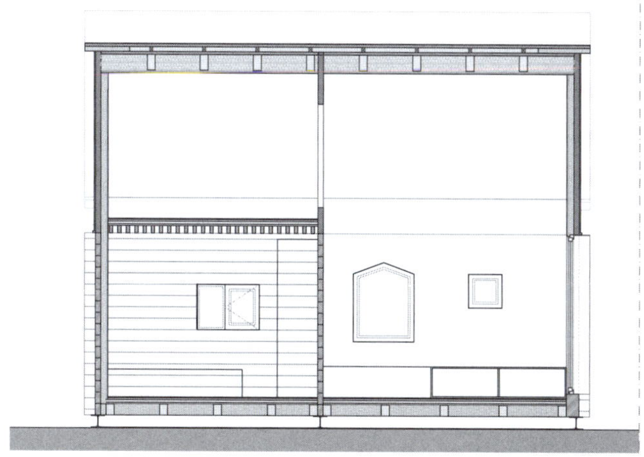

d e

b Side view of the chalet with snow.
Seitenansicht Chalet mit Schnee.

c Interior view of the attic floor.
Innenansicht Dachgeschoss.

d First floor plan.
Grundriss Erdgeschoss.

e Longitudinal section.
Längsschnitt.

f Pro-tò-ti-po 1:1 in the midst of nature.
Pro-tò-ti-po 1:1 inmitten der Natur.

f

Mezi Lukami
Between Meadows

Čeladná
Czech Republic

Completion: 2021
Area: 260 m²
Number of Rooms: 6
Photos: Romana Bennet

Between Meadows was created after restoring a historic log cabin. The reconstruction is characterized by a respectful approach to traditional craftsmanship, materials, and the site. Both understated simplicity and lovely details, such as its carved beams filled with sheep fleece, or the roof covered with hand-chopped larch shingles, are striking. The floors made of centuries-old stones are combined with contemporary furnishings to great effect.

Between Meadows entstand nach der Restaurierung einer historischen Blockhütte. Der respektvolle Umgang mit den traditionellen Handwerkstechniken, den Materialien und dem Ort prägen den Wiederaufbau. Hier überraschen sowohl die schlichte Einfachheit als auch die liebevollen Details wie geschnitzte Balken, die mit Schafsvlies gefüllt sind oder das mit handgehackten Lärchenschindeln belegte Dach. Die Fußböden aus jahrhundertealten Steinen wurden wirkungsvoll mit aktuellem Mobiliar kombiniert.

a **Cozy living room with old stone.** Gemütliches Wohnzimmer mit altem Naturstein.

b **View of the passageway with the moon lamp.** Blick auf den Durchgang mit der Mondlampe.

a b

c d

e f

c Detail of the wood staircase in the living area.
Detail Holztreppe im Wohnbereich.

d Kitchenarea.
Küchenbereich.

e Passageway between house and barn.
Durchgang zwischen Haus und Scheune.

f Bedroom with old plank floor.
Schlafzimmer mit altem Dielenboden.

g First floor and second floor plans.
Grundrisse Erdgeschoss und 1. Obergeschoss.

h Exterior view Mezi Lukami with its original stone façade.
Außenansicht Mezi Lukami mit der ursprünglichen Steinfassade.

g

h

Kvitfjell Cabin

Kvitfjell
Norway

Completion: 2021
Area: 145 m²
Number of Rooms: 8
Photos: Alejandro Villanueva

Nestled in the landscape on the top of Kvitfjell, this narrow chalet extends over 26 meters. It is made in accordance with traditional construction methods from local pine wood. The exterior walls and roof are clad in untreated wood panels that will naturally turn gray over time. Interior walls, ceilings and floors are made of white oiled pine wood to keep the rooms bright during dark winter days. All main rooms face southwest in accordance with the position of the sun. Respecting the topography of the site, the main living spaces and bathroom with vaulted ceilings are lowered into the landscape.

Eingebettet in die Landschaft auf dem Gipfel des Kvitfjell erstreckt sich dieses schmale Chalet über 26 Meter. Das Chalet wurde in traditioneller Bauweise aus heimischem Kiefernholz errichtet. Die Außenwände und das Dach sind mit unbehandelten Holzplatten verkleidet, die mit der Zeit natürlich vergrauen. Innenwände, Decken und Böden sind aus weiß geöltem Kiefernholz gefertigt – so bleiben die Räume in den dunklen Winterstunden hell. Entsprechend des Sonnenstandes sind alle Haupträume nach Südwesten ausgerichtet. Der Topographie des Grundstücks folgend, sind die Hauptwohnräume und das Bad mit gewölbten Decken in die Landschaft abgesenkt.

a **Interior view of the wood kitchen with peninsula.**
Innenansicht der Küche aus Holz mit Halbinsel.

a

b c

d

b **Detail of the window overlooking the landscape.**
Detail des Fensters mit Blick auf die Außenlandschaft.

c **Exterior view from the east façade.**
Außenansicht von der Ostfassade.

d **Kvitfjell Cabin and surroundings from above.**
Kvitfjell Cabin und Umgebung von oben.

e **Floor plan.**
Grundriss.

f **Interior view of the dining and living area.**
Innenansicht Ess- und Wohnbereich.

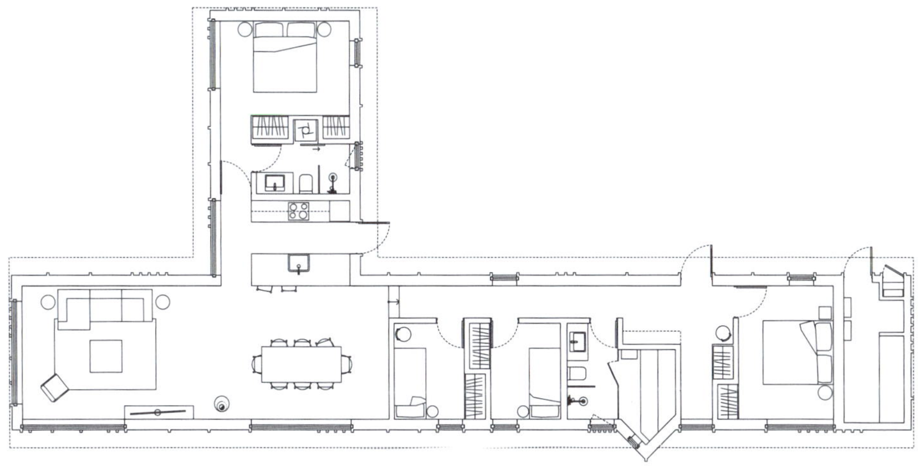

e

f

Hof Neuhäusl

Scheffau
Austria

Completion: 2017
Area: 148 m²
Number of Rooms: 5
Photos: David Schreyer
and Hans Peter Gruber

Demolition or renovation – fortunately, the client opted for the latter. Thus, a beautiful, accurately designed chalet with a great cozy atmosphere awoke from its Sleeping Beauty slumber. The exterior appearance of the old farmhouse was preserved, while inside the rooms were restructured to meet the highest modern living standards and offer its new users the highest level of comfort. Heating the property efficiently via a heat pump compact unit is possible thanks to the compactness of the existing cubature, ultra-low heating needs and the use of the most advanced building materials.

Abriss oder Sanierung – Dankenswerterweise hat sich der Bauherr für zweiteres entschieden. So konnte ein wunderschönes, präzise gestaltetes Chalet mit viel wohliger Atmosphäre aus dem Dornröschenschlaf geweckt werden. Das äußere Erscheinungsbild des alten Bauernhauses blieb erhalten, im Inneren wurden die Räume neu strukturiert, um höchsten, modernen Wohnansprüchen gerecht werden zu können und seinen neuen Nutzern höchste Behaglichkeit zu bieten. Aufgrund der Kompaktheit der vorhandenen Kubatur, dem sehr geringen Heizenergiebedarf und dem Einsatz modernster Baustoffe ist die Beheizung des Objekts über ein Wärmepumpekompaktgerät effizient möglich.

a **Interior view of the dining area with wooden corner bench.** Innenansicht Essbereich mit Eckbank aus Holz.

a

b

c

b **View from the living room toward the kitchen and gallery.**
Blick vom Wohnzimmer Richtung Küche und Galerie.

c **Exterior view from the south in the direction of the Kaisergebirge.**
Außenansicht von Süden Richtung Kaisergebirge.

d **First and second floor plans.**
Grundrisse Erdgeschoss und Obergeschoss.

e **View from the kitchen towards the living room.**
Blick von der Küche in Richtung Wohnzimmer.

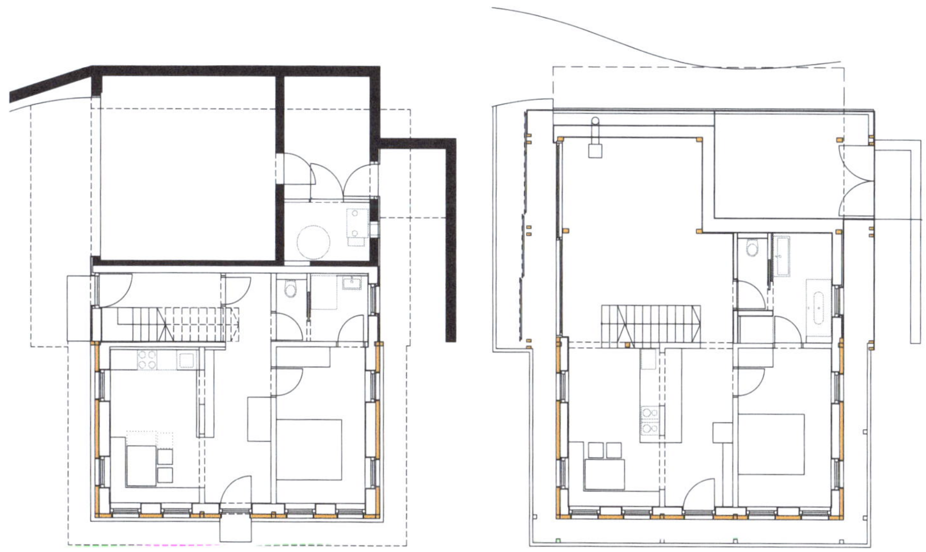

d

e

Forest DublDom

New Moscow
Russia

Completion: 2021
Area: 202 m²
Number of Rooms: 3
Photos: Arseny Rossikhin
and Ivan Ovchinnikov

The chalet Forest DublDom in the heart of the woods harmonizes with its surroundings and becomes part of nature. This works through its special basement design: due its many passages and niches, the house looks as if it stands out from the ground. This creates an interplay of light and shadow, closed and open spaces alternate, corridors and storage rooms are oriented to existing trunks. Another design feature is the house's windows opening views over the treetops. The chalet's interior is designed around the windows and focuses on the view, giving the impression of living in a tree house.

Das Chalet Forest DublDom mitten im Wald harmoniert mit seiner Umgebung und wird Teil der Natur. Das gelingt auch durch die besondere Gestaltung des Kellers: Durch viele Durchgänge und Nischen entsteht der Eindruck, dass sich das Haus vom Boden abhebt. Es entsteht ein Spiel aus Licht und Schatten, geschlossene und offene Räume wechseln sich ab, Gänge und Lagerräume sind an den vorhandenen Baumstämmen orientiert. Ein weiterer Fokus liegt auf den Fenstern im Haus, die den Blick auf die Baumkronen freigeben. Das Interieur ist um die Fenster herum konstruiert und stellt den Ausblick in den Mittelpunkt, so dass der Eindruck entsteht, in einem Baumhaus zu wohnen.

a **Interior view of the living room with fireplace and view of the forest.**
Innenansicht Wohnzeimmer mit Kamin und Blick auf den Wald.

a

b

c

b **Exterior view at night.**
Außenansicht bei Nacht.

c **Dining and living area with panoramic window.**
Ess- und Wohnbereich mit Panoramafenster.

d **First and second floor plans.**
Grundrisse Erdgeschoss und Obergeschoss.

e **Interior view of the bedroom.**
Innenansicht Schlafzimmer.

d

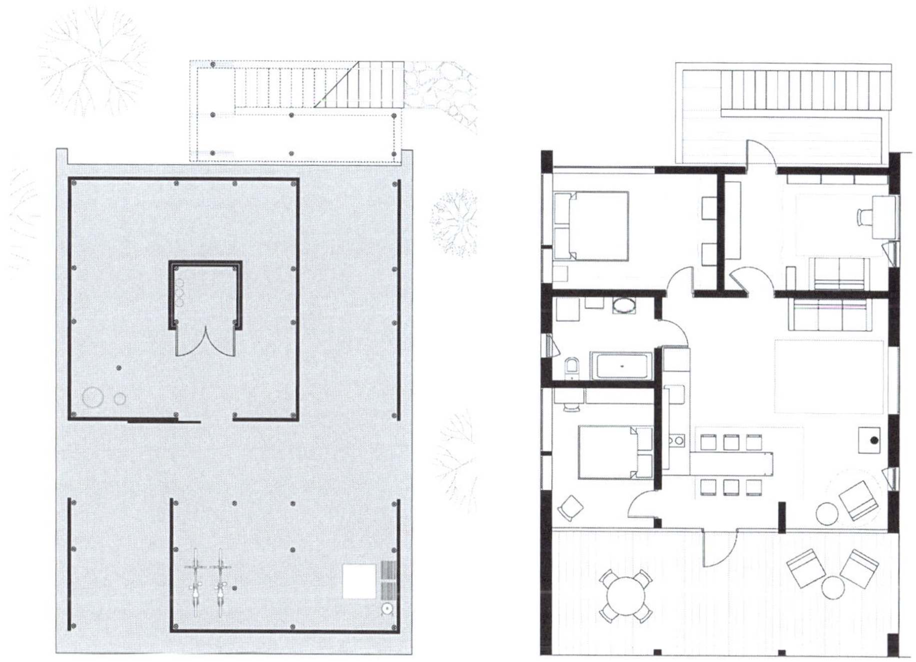

e

Chalet La

Pyrenees France

Completion: 2021
Area: 126 m²
Number of Rooms: 6
Photos: Lorenzo Zandri

Chalet La provides a breath-taking view of the mountain range Cambre d'Aze and the neighbouring lake. Following the site's slope, the space is divided into three levels, all facing the lake. The master bedroom located under the rafters as well as the living area on the ground floor, which is connected to the terrace, both benefit from a panoramic window that not only provides natural light but also blurs the line between inside and outside. Walls and ceilings are clad in timber, and the use of raw materials such as natural stone, concrete and steel makes for a mix of vintage hut style and industrial touches.

Das Chalet La bietet einen atemberaubenden Blick auf die Bergkette Cambre d'Aze und auf den benachbarten See. Dem vorhandenen Gefälle des Grundstücks folgend ist der Raum in drei Ebenen unterteilt, die alle auf den See ausgerichtet sind. Das Hauptschlafzimmer unter den Dachsparren und der Wohnbereich im Erdgeschoss, der mit der Terrasse verbunden ist, profitieren beide von einem Panoramafenster, das nicht nur natürliches Licht bietet, sondern auch die Grenze zwischen Innen und Außen verwischt. Wände und Decken sind mit Holz verkleidet, die Verwendung von Rohstoffen wie Naturstein, Beton und Stahl sorgt für eine Mischung aus altem Hüttencharakter und industriellen Akzenten.

a **Interior view of living room with fireplace.**
Innenansicht Wohnzimmer mit Kamin.

a

b c

d

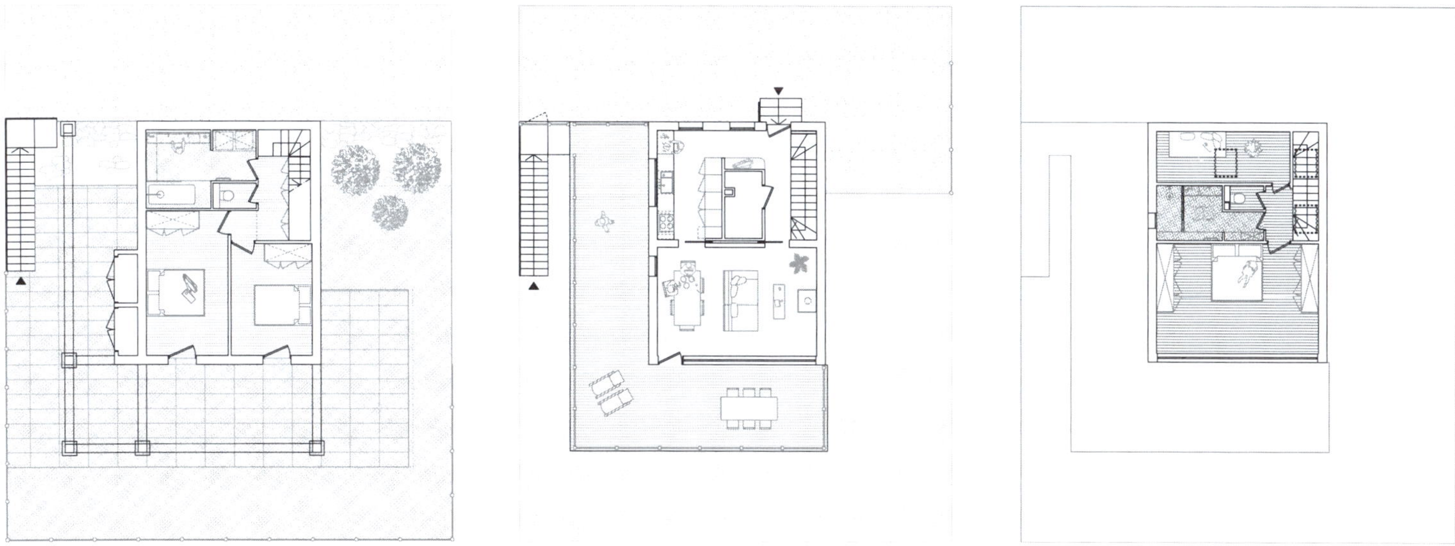

e f g

b Interior view with a skylight window.
Innenansicht mit Oberlichtfenster.

c Chalet master bedroom.
Hauptschlafzimmer Chalet.

d Dining room with vertical windows.
Esszimmer mit vertikalen Fenstern.

e First floor plan.
Grundriss Erdgeschoss.

f Second floor plan.
Grundriss 1. Obergeschoss.

g Attic floor plan.
Grundriss Dachgeschoss.

h Panoramic view of the mountains from the terrace.
Panoramablick auf die Berge von der Terrasse.

h

Mountain Hut

Krkonoše Mountains Czech Republic

Completion: 2019
Area: 200 m²
Number of Rooms: 5
Photos: a1architects/ David Maštálka

Mountain Hut is conceived as a modest and simple building. From top, the chalet is almost hidden and absorbed by a meadow. Just beneath the hill, reveals its wooden face on a plinth made of local stones found in the area. The interior is mainly made of light-colored wood. Family and friends gather at the large table and around the stove at the ground floor. This is also where the principal bedroom and the entire house's service area are located. The attic offers additional rooms for guests and children and a spacious common room with a view over the large valley.

Mountain Hut ist als ein bescheidenes und schlichtes Gebäude konzipiert. Von oben gesehen ist das Chalet fast versteckt und in der Wiese versunken. Unter dem Hügel öffnet sich sein hölzernes Gesicht auf dem Sockel aus lokalen Steinen, die in der Umgebung gefunden wurden. Helles Holz dominiert den Innenausbau. Im Erdgeschoss versammeln sich die Familie und ihre Freunde am großen Tisch und um den Ofen. Hier befindet sich auch das Hauptschlafzimmer und der gesamte Servicebereich des Hauses. Im Dachgeschoss finden sich weitere Schlafzimmer für Gäste und Kinder und ein großzügiger Gemeinschaftsraum mit Blick auf das große Tal.

a **Recreation and playroom on the second floor.**
Freizeit- und Spielraum im Obergeschoss.

a

b

c

b Main living and dining room with large stove.
Hauptwohn- und Esszimmer mit großem Ofen.

c Covered terrace with sliding glass door.
Überdachte Terrasse mit Glasschiebetür.

d First floor plan.
Grundriss Erdgeschoss.

e Second floor plan.
Grundriss 1. Obergeschoss.

f Exterior view of the chalet with Panoramic view.
Außenansicht des Chalets mit Panoramablick.

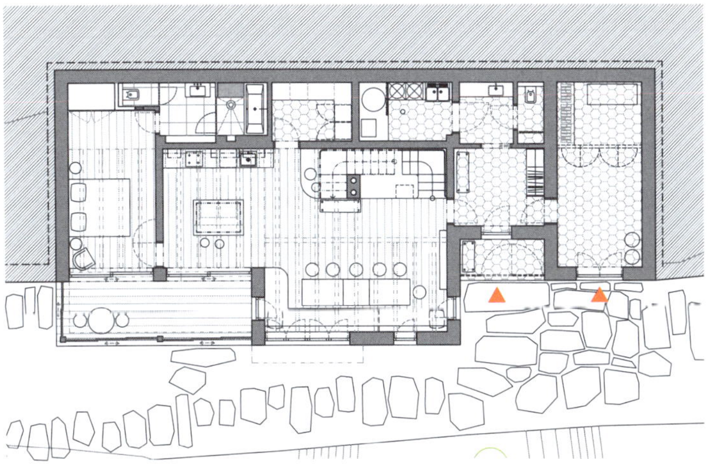

d

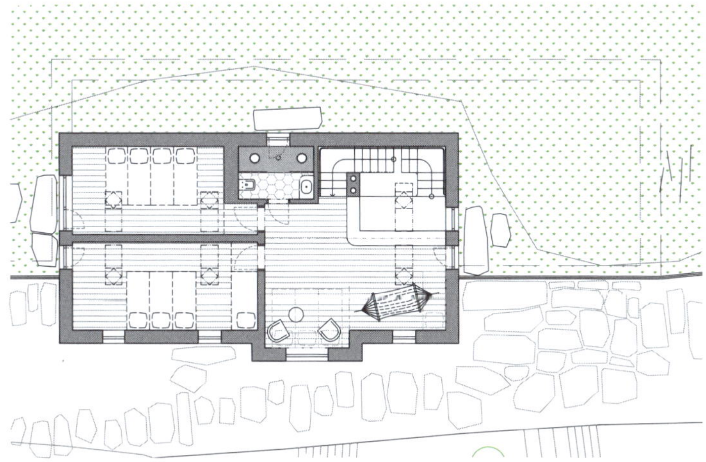

e

f

Messner House

Seis
Italy

Completion: 2017
Area: 220 m²
Number of Bedrooms: 3
Photos: Alex Filz

Below the Schlern mountain, a barn is given a new lease of life as a house. The project is based on South Tyrolean tradition and surprises with its visionary and most unexpected interior design. Seeking dialogue with tradition, but at the same time breaking away from it to define its own identity. This was the challenge faced during the process of developing the new house in Siusi allo Sciliar. The result is a building with two opposing souls. From the outside, a traditional house in the Alps that blends into the surrounding landscape. And inside, the surprise of a space without clichés: permeable and innovative.

Am Fuße des Schlern wird ein Stadel als Haus zu neuem Leben erweckt. Das Projekt orientiert sich an Südtiroler Tradition und überrascht mit seiner visionären und unerwarteten Inneneinrichtung. Den Dialog mit der Tradition suchen, sich aber gleichzeitig von ihr lösen, um die eigene Identität zu definieren. Das war die Herausforderung bei der Entwicklung des neuen Hauses in Seis am Schlern. Das Ergebnis ist ein Gebäude mit zwei entgegengesetzten Seelen. Von außen ein traditionelles Haus in den Alpen, das sich in die umliegende Landschaft eingliedert. Und innen die Überraschung eines Raums ohne Klischees: durchlässig und innovativ.

a **Interior view of the kitchen, dining and living room.**
Innenansicht Küche, Ess- und Wohnbereich.

a

b c

d

b **Interior view with skylight and mountain view.**
Innenansicht mit Oberlicht und Bergblick.

c **Kitchen and dining area with fireplace.**
Küche und Essbereich mit Kaminofen.

d **Exterior view from the street.**
Außenansicht von der Straße.

e **Messner House longitudinal section.**
Längsschnitt Messner House.

f **View from below.**
Blick von unten.

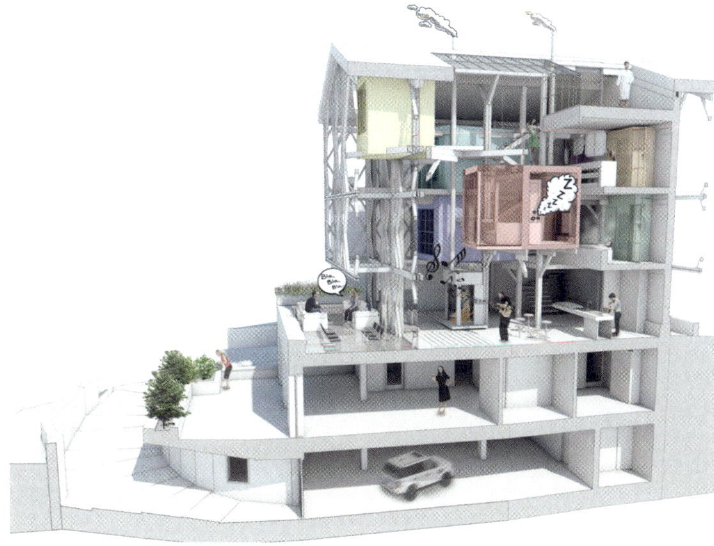

e

f

Cabin Son

Oslofjord Norway

Completion: 2020
Area: 70 m²
Number of Rooms: 5
Photos: Øystein Aspelund

The all-season chalet overlooking the island of Jeløya in the Oslofjord is about an hour from Oslo. The building is placed on natural rocky ledges in steep terrain in a way to seal it from the road on the one hand and open it to nature on the other. That way, design satisfies the need for privacy and, at the same time, opens up the fantastic view of the sea. Inspired by the small pre-existing building, the new construction is based on the original in terms of orientation and choice of materials, creating an independent chalet on several levels that meets all the needs of its users.

Das ganzjährig nutzbare Chalet mit Blick auf die Insel Jeløya im Oslofjord liegt ca. eine Stunde von Oslo entfernt. Das Gebäude ist so auf den natürlich vorkommenden Felsvorsprüngen in steilem Gelände platziert, dass es sich einerseits zur Straße verschließt und andererseits zur Natur hin öffnet. So wird der Entwurf dem Bedürfnis nach Privatsphäre gerecht und gibt gleichzeitig den phantastischen Blick auf das Meer frei. Inspiriert von dem kleinen, vorhandenen Gebäude, orientiert sich der Neubau in seiner Ausrichtung und Materialität am Bestand und schafft auf mehreren Ebenen ein eigenständiges Chalet, das allen Ansprüchen seiner Nutzer gerecht wird.

a **View of the bedroom with panoramic window and hallway with a climbing wall.**
Blick auf das Schlafzimmer mit Panoramafenster und den Flur mit Kletterwand.

a

b

c

b **Exterior view of Cabin Son at night.**
Außenansicht Cabin Son bei Nacht.

c **Interior view of the dining and living area with view of the surroundings.**
Innenansicht Ess- und Wohnbereich mit Blick auf die Umgebung.

d **Floor plan and cross sections.**
Grundriss und Querschnitte.

e **Detail of the roof overhang and large windows.**
Detail des Dachüberstands und der großen Fenster.

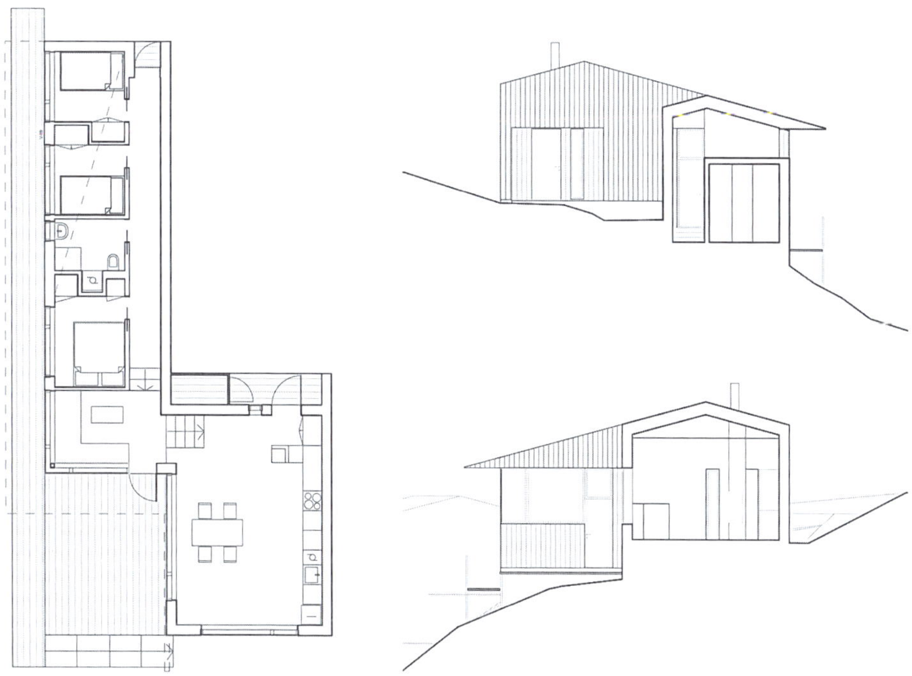

d

e

Haus am Berg

South Tyrol Italy

Completion: 2019
Area: 145 m²
Number of Rooms: 6
Photos: Davide Perbellini

Haus am Berg is a private house with a particular style built according to ecological principles. The goal was to reinterpret the traditional alpine chalet. Despite the small building volume, generous, light-flooded rooms were created inside. The openings and large windows are placed in a way that the surrounding nature is part of the interior and generate unique lighting moods. The simplicity and minimalism of the interior design results from the solid timber structure, which is still visible in the interior, in combination with a small number of clay plaster walls. By adding personalized furnishings and natural textiles, the home feels in harmony and timeless.

Das Haus am Berg ist ein baubiologisches Privathaus mit eigenem Charakter. Das architektonische Ziel war die Neuinterpretation einer Almhütte. Trotz des geringen Bauvolumens entstanden im Inneren großzügige, lichtdurchflutete Räume. Durch gezielt gesetzte Öffnungen und große Fenster wird die umliegende Natur Teil des Raumes und es entstehen einzigartige Lichtstimmungen. Das Massivholz der Konstruktion wurde im Inneren sichtbar gelassen und bildet in Kombination mit einigen in Lehm verputzten Wänden ein schlichtes und reduziertes Interior Design. Gepaart mit persönlichen Einrichtungsstücken und natürlichen Textilien entsteht ein harmonisches, zeitlos-modernes Zuhause.

a **Dining area with balcony and panoramic view.**
Essbereich mit Balkon und Panoramablick.

a

b

c

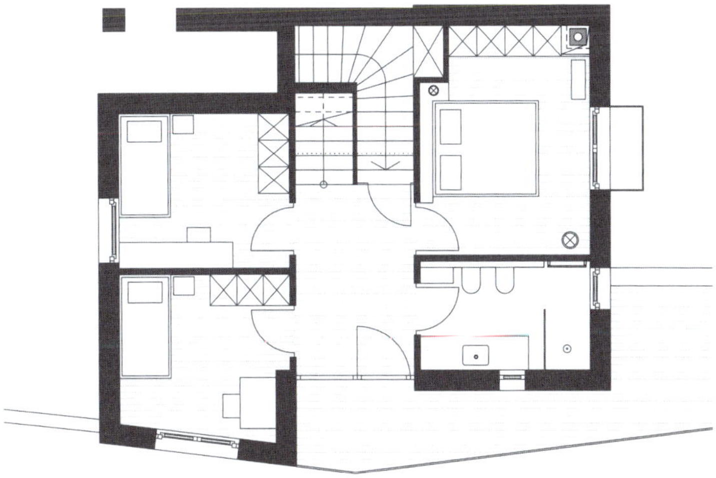

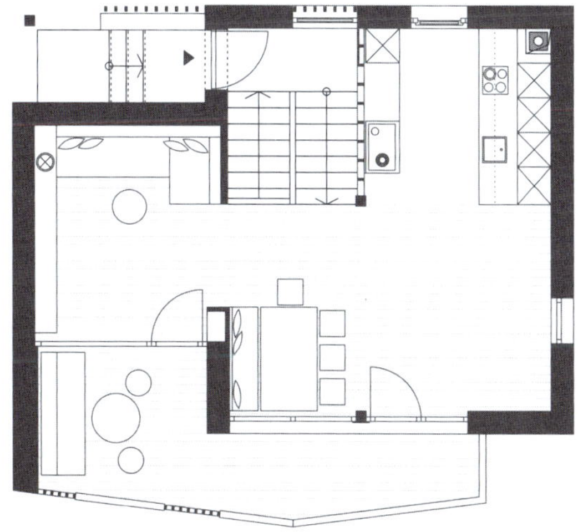

d e

b View into the kitchen area.
Blick in den Küchenbereich.

c Exterior view Haus am Berg from the garden.
Außenansicht Haus am Berg vom Garten.

d First floor plan.
Grundriss Erdgeschoss.

e Attic floor plan.
Grundriss Dachgeschoss.

f Interior view with a long vertical window.
Innenansicht mit langem vertikalem Fenster.

f

Bundwerkstadel Aubenhausen

Tuntenhausen
Germany

Completion: 2019
Area: 800 m^2
Number of Rooms: 12
Photos: Jonathan Sage

The 250-year-old Bundwerkstadel was converted into a seminar and residential building. The Bundwerkstadel's wooden structure is fully glazed and thus can be experienced from inside the building. Vertical wooden slats give the exterior an easy and calm look. A three-story sculpture of stacked wooden cubes divides the interior space and makes it possible to fully enjoy the barn "up to the roof". Surfaces of light silver fir contrast with dark old wood in a subtle way. The "Tennen" as historic passageways are kept free of installations except light bridges and footbridges and visually connect with the outside space through huge glass gates.

Der 250 Jahre alte Bundwerkstadel wurde in ein Seminar- und Wohnhaus umgenutzt. Die Innenseite des Bundwerks wurde vollflächig verglast und damit aus dem Innenraum erlebbar. Vertikale Holzlatten beruhigen die Außenansicht. Eine dreigeschossige Skulptur aus gestapelten Holzkuben schafft die Raumaufteilung im Inneren und macht den Stadel „bis unters Dach" erlebbar. Oberflächen aus heller Weißtanne bilden einen unaufdringlichen Kontrast zum dunklen Altholz. Die „Tennen" als historische Durchfahrten bleiben bis auf leichte Brücken und Stege frei von Einbauten und verbinden sich durch riesige Glastore optisch mit dem Außenraum.

a

a **Interior view of the southern passageways with surfaces of silver fir and aged timber.**
Innenansicht südliche Tenne mit Weißtanneoberflächen und Altholz.

b

c d

b **Exterior view of the southern threshing floor with snow.**
Außenansicht der südlichen Tenne mit Schnee.

c **Interior view glazed room behind Bundwerk.**
Innenansicht verglastes Zimmer hinter Bundwerk.

d **Stairway view of the southern threshing floor.**
Blick zur Treppe im südlichen Tenne.

e **First, second and attic floor plans.**
Grundrisse Erdgeschoss, Obergeschoss and Dachgeschoss.

f **View to the south with morning atmosphere.**
Blick nach Süden mit Morgenstimmung.

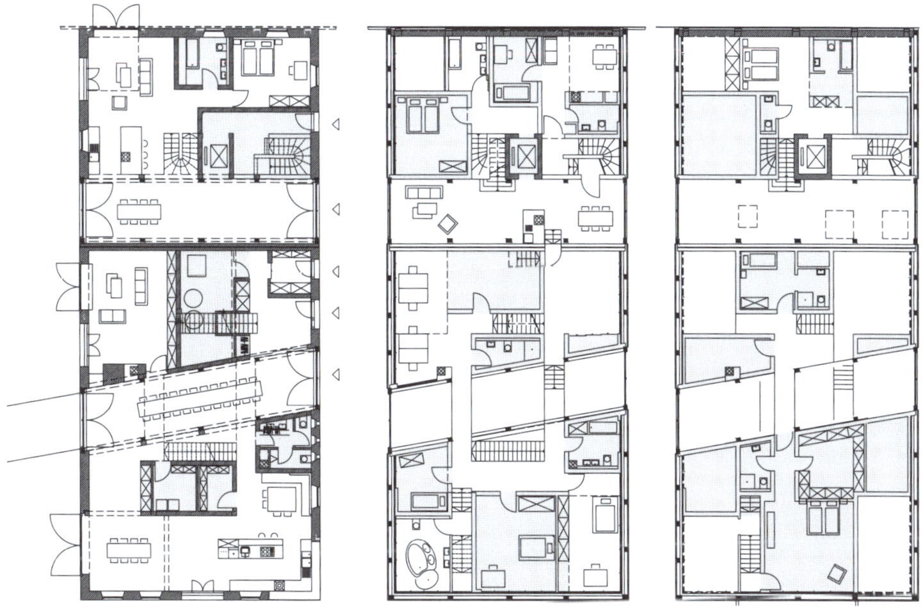

e

f

Architects + Studios

Architekten + Büros

Imprint

The Deutsche Nationalbibliothek lists this publication in the Deutsche Nationalbibliografie; detailed bibliographic data are available on the Internet at http://dnb.dnb.de

ISBN 978-3-03768-280-7

www.braun-publishing.ch

1st edition 2024

Editor: Sibylle Kramer
Editorial staff and layout: Alessia Calabrò
Translation: Sandra Ellegiers
Graphic concept: Eva Finkbeiner
Reproduction: Bild1Druck GmbH, Berlin

All of the information in this volume has been compiled to the best of the editor's knowledge. It is based on the information provided to the publisher by the architects' and designers' offices and excludes any liability. The publisher assumes no responsibility for its accuracy or completeness as well as copyright discrepancies and refers to the specified sources (architects' and designers' offices as well as hosts). All rights to the photographs are property of the photographer (please refer to the picture credits)

Editor's comment:
This book has been translated into American English. In American English, the floor at street level is called the second floor. If you go up one floor, you are on the second floor accordingly. The floor below street level is called the basement.

Die Deutsche Nationalbibliothek verzeichnet diese Publikation in der Deutschen Nationalbibliografie; detaillierte bibliografische Daten sind im Internet über http://dnb.dnb.de abrufbar.

ISBN 978-3-03768-280-7

www.braun-publishing.ch

1. Auflage 2024

Redaktion: Sibylle Kramer
Mitarbeit Redaktion und Layout: Alessia Calabrò
Übersetzung: Sandra Ellegiers
Grafisches Konzept: Eva Finkbeiner
Reproduktion: Bild1Druck GmbH, Berlin

Alle Informationen in diesem Band wurden mit dem besten Gewissen der Redaktion zusammengestellt. Das Buch basiert auf den Informationen, die der Verlag von Architekten-und Designbüros erhielt und schließt jegliche Haftung aus. Der Verlag übernimmt keine Verantwortung für die Richtigkeit und Vollständigkeit sowie Urheberrechte und verweist auf die angegebenen Quellen (Architekten- und Designbüros sowie Betreiber). Alle Rechte an den Fotografien sind im Besitz der Fotografen (siehe Abbildungsnachweise).

Anmerkung der Redaktion:
Dieses Buch wurde ins amerikanische Englisch übersetzt. Im amerikanischen Englisch wird das Stockwerk auf der Straßenebene als erster Stock bezeichnet. Geht man eine Etage höher, befindet man sich entsprechend im zweiten Stock. Die Etage unterhalb der Straßenebene wird Keller genannt.